WATCHING
MONTY

WATCHING MONTY

THE EVERYDAY LIFE OF
GENERAL BERNARD MONTGOMERY

JOHNNY HENDERSON WITH JAMIE DOUGLAS-HOME
FOREWORD BY SIR CAROL MATHER MC

IMPERIAL WAR MUSEUM

First published 2005
This paperback edition first published 2024

The History Press
97 St George's Place, Cheltenham,
Gloucestershire, GL50 3QB
www.thehistorypress.co.uk

In association with the Imperial War Museum

Text © The Estate of J.R. Henderson, Jamie Douglas-Home, 2005, 2024
Imperial War Museum photographs © The Imperial War Museum, 2005, 2024

British Library Cataloguing in Publication Data.
A catalogue record for this book is available from the British Library.

ISBN 978 1 80399 630 1

Typesetting and origination by The History Press
Printed and bound in Great Britain by TJ Books Limited, Padstow, Cornwall

Trees for LYfe

CONTENTS

FOREWORD

BY SIR CAROL MATHER MC

I first met Johnny Henderson at Monty's Tac HQ immediately after the victorious Battle of Alamein. I was acting as Monty's liaison officer; Johnny had arrived as his new ADC. But the roles were interchangeable. Henderson, although a young officer, was an experienced desert hand. I was sure he would be okay. So I showed him into his bivvy tent and left. I was departing for an ill-fated SAS raid behind the lines.

I was not to see him again for the best part of a year. After I had been captured and taken prisoner of war, I made a beeline for Monty's Tac HQ following a lucky escape through enemy lines in Southern Italy. Monty was away. Johnny was in charge and put my companion and myself to sleep in Monty's caravans. What a contrast from the moaning of the oxen in some godforsaken barn a few nights earlier. Once the invasion of Europe began, I was invited to rejoin Montgomery in my former role. Henderson was by now his longstanding ADC.

It was like old times serving at Monty's Tac HQ. One was right at the heart of the action; contrary to the usual perception, he was a very relaxed and easy master, but only if he trusted you. If he did not, you were out. Of course, he had a ruthless streak, particularly with officers, of whatever rank, whom he considered 'useless'. He liked to relax in the company of his young staff, as Johnny's memoirs make clear, and, in the mess, was always goading them to admit youthful indiscretions. But no cheekiness in return was expected! I cannot imagine a happier atmosphere at any similar command post. And his use of liaison officers was a touch of brilliance. But Monty was inclined to be jealous or dismissive when it came to his army contemporaries. The exceptions being his own army and corps commanders and, of course, Brooke and Alexander.

Johnny's rapport with Monty played a little known but crucial part in the winning of the war; for here was someone upon whose absolute loyalty he could depend and who was also an agreeable companion (Monty tolerated Johnny's somewhat impish sense of humour). Whatever the location – in the deserts of North Africa, across the Italian plains and mountains, in Normandy, or even on Lüneburg Heath at the time of the Surrender – Johnny, as his aide, laid out Monty's little tented camp, exactly as it had been at Alamein. It is not sour grapes to recall that American generals opted for the largest château available!

I am glad that Johnny Henderson finally decided to tell his side of the story, for it is laced with humour. On many occasions he can be seen to be skating on very thin ice, but, when found out, Monty took it in very good part. What these pages reveal is the human face of war: both of a great commander, and of his shrewd but modest ADC. A double act, if you like, but a very good one.

PROLOGUE

When I left Monty in 1946 after being his ADC for nearly four years, he said, 'Johnny, you must never write a book.' Then he added, 'Anyhow, you are not capable of it.' Actually I have never before been inclined to do so. But now, some sixty years later, I have decided to tell some stories of my time with Monty before it is too late. I do so at the suggestion of a few friends. Perhaps it is presumptive to refer to my efforts as a book!

Memory is kind. It tends to recall the more amusing times and forget so many of the long, drearier days and some of the more alarming moments. Monty's brilliant military exploits and his great battles have been extensively documented. So I hope my reminiscences will give an idea of the less well-known but lighter side of Monty's Tac HQ (Tactical Headquarters) and the relaxed atmosphere in which we lived. I have also included many photographs from personal albums that I put together at the time.

As I am nearly the only fellow still around who was close to Monty at the time, I have given interviews to two German television stations recently. They asked me if I saluted every time I saw Monty and if I always called him 'Sir'. I replied that I did not think I had ever saluted him and that, after the first week or so, I never called him 'Sir' again. They could hardly believe their ears and were amazed to learn that life with Monty was nothing like as austere as they had previously thought.

I left Eton in the beginning of 1939 and was just about to go up to Cambridge to study history at Trinity when war was declared. I was at the university for a year, but it was an unsatisfactory time, as everyone wanted to get off to the war and one never really knew if one would be going back for the next term or not.

In the summer of 1940, while I was waiting to join the Coldstream Guards, I happened to go back to Eton for the Fourth of June celebrations and met an old friend, Kenneth Inchcape, who had just got back from Dunkirk. Kenneth said, 'Why don't you join a cavalry regiment instead and come to my lot, the 12th Lancers?' The idea rather appealed to me, so Kenneth promised that he would sound out the colonel. He must have given me a reasonable reference because I soon heard that the 12th Royal Lancers had accepted me. Then I was called up the following week.

I went to Farnborough as a private soldier to learn the ropes for about a month and then moved on to Sandhurst to be trained as an officer. Four months later I joined my new regiment, which was based near Horsham in Sussex, preparing for a possible invasion.

I had been there nearly a year when we heard that we were going to be sent to the war in Egypt. In late 1941 we set sail in the last ship in a large convoy. I remember we had to sleep in our lifejackets because the U-boats were on the prowl.

Eventually we got round the Cape and disembarked in Durban on 3 November. After two weeks or so there, we were transferred to another ship, *The New Amsterdam*, which was reputed to go much faster than the enemy submarines. I believe there were something like 22,000 troops on her. Therefore we had to take turns in the hammocks, as there was not enough room for everyone to sleep at the same time. It was very hot and uncomfortable, but the ship only took three or four days to get up to the Suez Canal.

We stayed near Cairo to start with and were sent out to join the battle in the desert in December 1941. Auchinleck's front line was then deep into Libya, but we were soon forced to retreat. Rommel gradually pushed us further and further back and, by July 1942, the enemy was only 60 miles or so from Alexandria.

For some reason I was able to find my way around the desert using a sun compass. So, around that time, I was chosen to take a convoy of three armoured cars and five supply vehicles to see if we could get across the Qattara Depression, a large and virtually uncharted area of salt lakes and marshes about 30 miles south of Alamein. The idea was to find out if the enemy could creep through the depression and then launch a surprise attack on the Alamein line of defences.

It soon became clear that a large force would have no hope of completing such a task. Our vehicles were only able to travel a short distance of two or three hundred yards before one would invariably break the thick salt crust that covered the bog and get stuck. We would then dig it out and continue on our way. It was a tiresome process, but in the end we managed to cross the marshes and, a little further on, we came upon a narrow path leading up a steep escarpment.

Monty's Tac HQ camp in the desert. (Eton College Library)

As we were now a long way behind enemy lines, I told the drivers of the vehicles to wait while I took my jeep up the path to explore.

I had not gone very far when I spotted a German tank coming towards me with some of its crew lying, sunbathing, on the top. Luckily, I found a spot wide enough to turn the jeep round, and, hooting my horn continuously to warn the others at the bottom, set off down the track with the tank in hot pursuit. They fired at us as if we were running rabbits, as we dispersed and rushed off into the desert.

Somehow we lost our pursuers, and when the convoy met up again we were delighted to discover that we had all emerged from the desperate chase unharmed. We then drove back over the marshes, using our old tracks to avoid getting stuck. As we could only move by night because German planes were out searching for us during the hours of daylight, it took a long time to get home. Indeed, when we arrived safely at our base, we had been away for two weeks.

A few months later my regiment fought on the southern flank during the famous battle of Alamein. Then, on 10 November 1942, less than a week after Monty's great victory, this rather surprised and extremely nervous captain of only 22 years old was summoned to join the triumphant Eighth Army commander's personal staff. I have always thought that the main reason why I got the job was because I managed to plot a course through those treacherous marshes twice.

Monty learned early on that I had no ambitions to be a regular soldier after the war. One night at dinner in the desert he asked me what I thought of a pamphlet he had written on army leadership. When I said that I had not read it, he exclaimed, 'Oh Johnny, you will never make a soldier.' 'You are quite right,' I replied, 'and, anyhow, I don't want to be one.' 'So what do you want to do?' he asked. When I said I wished to go into the City, Monty retorted, 'Oh, that's no good. All they want to do is make lots of money and put the dates of Ascot, Wimbledon and the start of the grouse shooting season into their diaries!' 'That,' I answered, 'is just what I want.'

Funnily enough, after I left the Army, my life panned out almost exactly as Monty had predicted. I had a long career in the City and racing and shooting became two of my favourite hobbies. But I still remained in close touch with my old chief, who kindly agreed to be godfather to my elder son, Nicky, and always used to come to lunch at our home near Newbury on the Sunday before Christmas.

INTRODUCTION

Lieutenant-General Bernard Law Montgomery, later Field-Marshal Viscount Montgomery of Alamein, was three months short of his 55th birthday when he set foot in Egypt in August 1942 as the new commander of the Eighth Army. I joined this remarkable individual that November and stayed with him for nearly four years. During that time I had practically every meal with Monty and lived with him day in day out. Therefore I saw every side of his character.

Monty was the most even-tempered person one could imagine. He hardly ever showed any emotion – not even on the morning of the Normandy landings or when he first heard that a German contingent was coming to surrender. About the only time I ever saw him agitated was in the early hours of 8 June 1944 (or D-Day +2 as it is also known) off the Normandy beaches when he told me to ask the captain of the destroyer, which had brought us over, to go in closer. He wanted to get ashore urgently and was upset when the boat shuddered as it hit the reef and it became clear that it could go no further.

Monty was a person who always wanted to be in command – yes, always. He made his opinions quite clear by repeating himself. He would listen on occasions to others, particularly his Chief of Staff, Freddie de Guingand, and his Head of Intelligence, Bill Williams. But, if something they had said changed his mind, he always claimed their ideas as if they were his own. I never heard Monty admit that he was wrong.

I have often been asked if he had a warm side. Yes, he did, but he was reluctant to show it. In the four years I was with him I never once heard him mention his wife, who had died just before the war. However, he was very proud of his son, David, and was always anxious to do for him what he felt was right. But, strangely, he also seemed to be jealous of anyone else giving David a good time.

Monty ended up with very few close personal friends after the war. He seemed unable to unwind outside Army circles. Sir Alan Herbert, the brilliant comic writer and MP for Oxford University, was a good friend of Monty and his wife, Betty, who knew many people in the world of the arts. Monty would ask A.P.H. out to Germany or Holland and his visits were the greatest fun for us. I remember in Luxembourg at the end of the war we had to find a piano for A.P.H. to play. Monty certainly enjoyed his performance. Monty was also close to another distinguished Oxford academic, the military historian, Professor Cyril Falls. Another true friend in peacetime was P.J. Grigg (Sir James Grigg, the Secretary of State for War during the war). But I cannot name another close confidant, who was not in the Army.

Bill Williams was once asked if Monty was a nice man. He replied, 'Nice men don't win wars.' That may be true but I thought Bill was being a little hard. Monty had a pleasant, straightforward sense of humour and liked the ridiculous. Although he did not much like humour against himself, he often told the following tale: when he was a colonel in the Royal Warwickshire Regiment in Egypt before the war, one of his young officers was permanently out with women and consequently too tired to be of service. So Monty got hold of the lad and said, 'I am giving you an order that you are not to go to bed with another woman without my permission, but in no circumstances must you be afraid to ask. See?'

Shortly afterwards, Monty was asked to dinner with the British Ambassador in Cairo. During dinner, the butler approached the Ambassador, bowed and said, 'There is a telephone call for Colonel Montgomery.' 'Ask who it is,' the Ambassador replied, 'and what he wants.' The butler soon returned: 'It is Lieutenant so and so asking his colonel if he can have a woman.' 'One woman once and back by ten' was Monty's curt reply.

Monty also had the ability to develop a clear picture of the most difficult situations. For instance, when his son got engaged, he was abroad, so he asked his father to take his fiancée to buy a ring. Monty realised that things could become tricky if she picked an item that was more expensive than David's budget of £250, so he visited a jeweller the day before his planned rendezvous with David's intended and told him to put all the rings worth £250 or below on to a single tray. It was then arranged that when Monty returned the next day with a pretty girl and asked to see his engagement rings, the jeweller would bring out the tray, saying it contained his complete collection. Monty could then be absolutely certain that a ring that was too dear would not be chosen!

Nigel Hamilton, who wrote a three-volume biography of Monty, suggested he was a repressed homosexual. I can truthfully say that such a thought never crossed my mind in the four years I was with him. Furthermore, if rumours had been circulating then, Monty's reputation would have been harmed and his credibility completely undermined. I can also swear that such a scenario never occurred. Hamilton says that he surrounded himself with young officers, but so did all his colleagues. Leese employed Ian Calvorcoressi, and Horrocks, Harold Young, as their ADCs, but nobody ever suggested those generals had homosexual tendencies. Monty wanted to command and it was much easier to order the young about. Moreover, his only relaxation was to have an argument at dinner each night – he could never have done that with a bunch of oldies!

Monty. (Imperial War Museum [IWM] TR1035)

I have also been asked if he was religious. Monty always had a Bible by his bedside, but I would not know how often he opened it. He would quite often say, 'Get on to Padre Hughes and tell him we want a service on Sunday. Not too long though.' We also had a wonderful Army chaplain in Europe whom Monty chose. So I suppose religion played a part in his life.

Monty did not much care what he ate, never drank alcohol, except a toast, but he never minded us having a dram. Before he left Germany to return to England to be Chief of the Imperial General Staff, he heard us saying that we might as well divide what bottles there were in the mess and take them back. He firmly reminded us, 'I am a member of this mess as much as any of you and I want my share.'

He was never concerned about what clothes he wore. In the desert, like everyone else, he would turn out in khaki shorts or trousers and an open-neck shirt. In Europe, he favoured corduroy trousers and a grey jersey. Even when Winston Churchill came he was seldom seen in uniform.

I have often been asked if I was fond of Monty. 'Fond' is a difficult word, and, in the past, I have never been able to answer yes or no. On reflection, I suppose that it would be unlikely for a 22–26-year-old, as I was then, to be fond of such a person. Yet, after all these years and having read what I have written, I think that I need no longer sit on the fence. I am now prepared to say that I was fond of this extraordinary character.

ONE

WITH THE EIGHTH ARMY IN THE DESERT
NOVEMBER 1942–JUNE 1943

When I joined Monty's Tac HQ, the Eighth Army was chasing Rommel's retreating forces into Libya and the Allied invasion of Morocco and Algeria under Eisenhower had just begun. So the depleted German and Italian Army was now facing a war on two fronts.

The Libyan port of Tobruk was recaptured on 12 November 1942. Then Monty won an important victory on 17 December at El Agheila on the coast road in between Benghazi and Tripoli, where some Eighth Army soldiers had been twice before. Monty then prepared to advance on Tripoli. We entered the Libyan capital on 23 January 1943 and stayed there for a few weeks to open up the harbour and build up our supplies for the next stage of the journey towards Tunis.

While we were in Tripoli, Rommel's attention turned to the other Allied front, and he attacked the Americans. The First Army was in considerable danger in late February, so Alexander, Eisenhower's Deputy Commander-in-Chief, asked Monty to put some pressure on the Afrika Korps from the other direction. Monty moved fast, and Rommel soon called off his assault on the Americans.

Monty guessed that Rommel's sights would now be set on the Eighth Army. As expected, the German commander attacked at Medenine inside the Tunisian border on 6 March. Rommel's forces were driven

Monty, dressed in his favourite casual attire. (IWM BM20753)

back, losing 52 tanks, but Monty declined to follow as the Germans withdrew. He knew that Rommel would stop at the great defensive obstacle, the Mareth Line, south of Gabes, which had been constructed by the French in case of an Italian attack from Tripolitania. Monty knew that the Mareth Line would be difficult to pierce and was ready for a hard fight. There were many anxious moments during the battle of a week, but a concerted blitz of air and ground forces on 27 March eventually won the day.

It was clear that the war in North Africa would finish soon, as the enemy was now hemmed in on both sides. Monty won a stiff one-day battle at Wadi Akarit, north of Gabes, on 6 April, and the Eighth Army joined up with the Americans, who were moving east from Gafsa, on 8 April. The city of Sfax was captured two days later. On 7 May the British forces took the capital, Tunis, and the Americans captured the port of Bizerte on Tunisia's northern tip. Six days later, on 13 May, all enemy forces surrendered and the Desert War was over.

My Arrival at the Eighth Army Tac HQ

It was 10 November 1942 and the historic battle of Alamein was over. The pursuit of the retreating German Army along the Egyptian coast towards the Libyan border was now on.

Left to right: *John Poston, Freddie de Guingand, Monty and the author, Johnny Henderson, in front of Tac HQ.* (Eton College Library)

My regiment, the 12th Royal Lancers, was part of the 1st Armoured Division and was not involved. So, for once, there was peace and quiet, but we always had to have our wirelesses ready for any orders from our squadron or, less likely, from regimental headquarters. My corporal arrived and said that there was a message to report to the colonel. We did not like these sorts of message as they invariably meant that we were to be sent on a nasty mission. The colonel, George Kidston, however, came quickly to the point, 'You are to go off to be ADC to the Army Commander.' 'Help, you mean, Monty' said I. 'Yes,' he replied. After a few minutes' thought, I asked if I could take Charlie Saunders, my wonderful soldier servant and, by now, friend with me.

Sidney Kirkman, who thought the author's new appointment was temporary. (Eton College LIbrary)

So we set off, full of apprehension, and got to the Eighth Army Tac HQ near Mersa Matruh about 4.30 p.m. As John Poston, his other ADC, was out with Monty, I waited in the mess tent, feeling mighty lonely. Then a senior officer walked in, whom I later discovered was Brigadier Kirkman. He said, 'Hello, are you the new temporary ADC?' That made me wonder how temporary my new appointment was to be!

Monty and John soon arrived. John introduced me to Monty, who, after a very short conversation, said, 'I will see you at dinner. John will look after you.' John had been ADC to General

'Strafer' Gott, who had been killed in an aeroplane crash soon after taking over command of the Eighth Army. Monty, of course, was Gott's successor.

Monty, Freddie de Guingand, Bill Williams, John and I dined together that evening. Dinner had hardly started when Monty began to fire questions at me. 'How long have you been in the desert? Why did you join the 12th Lancers? Where did you go to school?' 'Oh, Eton,' he exclaimed, 'and what do you say to that as John was at Harrow?' Well, I trotted out the usual old response: 'The one good thing about Harrow was that you could see Eton from it. Now, John, what about that?' That was the taste of dinner every night with Monty. He relaxed for an hour by starting an argument with us. We soon learnt we had to answer back.

I was glad when that ordeal was over, but, later that evening, John Poston gave me an invaluable bit of advice – to always tell the truth to Monty. If you did not and he found out, that was likely to be the end of you. So, John and I talked into the night in our beds in the tent let down off the side of Monty's caravan. John assured me that life there was much easier than I might have imagined.

Key Staff at Monty's Tac HQ in North Africa

Monty surrounded himself with a small number of key personal staff at his desert Tac HQ. I soon realised how efficiently they went about their business and also what a good picker of men the Eighth Army commander was.

Freddie de Guingand, who was 42 and then a brigadier, was already at Eighth Army HQ when Monty arrived in Egypt. Monty knew him previously and had always admired his ability. So he interviewed Freddie immediately and made him his Chief of Staff. Monty had decided to have a small forward HQ (Tac HQ) in order to be in close touch with the fighting line. He was determined that his experience as a divisional commander during the evacuation of Dunkirk in 1940 – communications broke down completely – should not be repeated. Also, as he was away from Main HQ, he did not get bogged down with unnecessary detail. Therefore Freddie was in charge of all that went on at Main HQ.

Bill Williams, Monty's head of intelligence. (Eton College Library)

Freddie was mighty clever, very quick and full of ideas – many of which Monty took on as his own. He lived on his nerves and consequently had health problems. But, unlike Monty, he appreciated the good things in life. As Freddie completely lacked pomposity, everyone, and I mean everyone, admired and loved him.

Monty had the amazing gift of simplifying any problem and making himself absolutely clear. So, when he made a plan, he always left Freddie to make the necessary arrangements. Freddie's talent for thinking of everything and putting a plan into action fast still makes the mind boggle. But, it made a huge difference that he was always cheerful and a friend to one and all.

Monty knew how lucky he was to have Freddie. Although he did not often sing men's praises, he did as far as Freddie was concerned. In fact, he later wrote, 'He was a brilliant Chief of Staff and I doubt if ever before such a one existed in the British Army or will ever do so again.'

Furthermore, because he was friendly with the American commander, Eisenhower, and Bedell Smith, Ike's Chief of Staff, Freddie smoothed over many a difficult situation. Indeed, I would go so far as to say that had it not been for Freddie's intervention, Monty might well have been relieved of his command in Europe in the tricky period in the autumn of 1944 after the liberation of Brussels.

Freddie spent half his time at the Tac HQ in the desert and had a caravan there. He would sit up in the evenings playing his favourite card game, *chemin de fer*, for small amounts of money. I never thought that a person in his position would become such a good friend in so short a time.

E.T. 'Bill' Williams, also a brigadier, was only 29 years old when he became Monty's Chief Staff Officer of Intelligence. But, as he was already at Eighth Army

Brian Robertson, a very efficient Q.
(Eton College LIbrary)

HQ, he was well known to Freddie. When the war started he was a don at Oxford and left to join the King's Dragoon Guards. Bill was a brilliantly clever fellow with a lovely dry sense of humour and told his stories in a lugubrious manner. He proved his value soon after Monty's arrival in Egypt by predicting when and where the Germans would attack at Alam Halfa. Every night he would wire John Poston or myself the all-important positions of the two German Panzer Divisions and their 90th Light Division.

In the early days Bill always took the press briefings. Immediately after the victory at Alamein, a huge crowd of reporters rushed round to his caravan and an American journalist said, 'Gee, this is the greatest thing that has happened in this area since the Crucifixion.' Bill replied, 'And it only took four to report on that.'

Bill had Monty's ear and the Army Commander relied on what he had to say and would listen intently. He played a huge part in the Eighth Army's victories. He came to see Monty once or twice a week and invariably stayed the night. Bill went back to England with Monty and was on his staff throughout the European campaign.

Brian Robertson, another brigadier, who was a lot older than us at 46, was a highly competent head of the Quartermaster's Department (Q). Brian, the son of a famous field-marshal, was a dry character but incredibly efficient. His instructions usually came from Freddie, but Monty knew he could rely on Brian.

When the Eighth Army advanced towards Tripoli, the lines of supply got longer and longer and the port of Benghazi further and further away. So Brian had a huge and complicated task, supplying the troops with food, ammunition, fuel and water. Also, as there were long delays at Benghazi, which was over 700 miles away from Tripoli, due to bad weather and the damage left by the retreating German Army, Brian's problems were exacerbated. For example, the supply of petrol on the long journey to Tripoli produced untold headaches. Brian, however, dealt with and overcame all these difficulties with masterly calmness.

Brian only came to visit once a fortnight, so Freddie always kept Monty fully informed if there were major problems at Q. Brian left the Eighth Army after Sicily to join Alexander's HQ. He took over from Monty as commander of the Rhine Army in the British Zone in occupied Germany in 1946 and later became head of the British Transport Commission, which was then responsible for the railways.

John Poston, a captain and Monty's ADC, suited him admirably. Although he was only 23, he had been fighting with his regiment, the 11th Hussars, for two years and knew his way round the desert. My ability to read a map and use a compass helped to get the job with Monty, but, as we knew each other in Northamptonshire before the war, John was also partly responsible for my appointment. So that was marvellous for me and John quickly became a great friend. He was full of self-confidence, very competent and always ready for a bit of fun. As John was the leader in our early escapades, life was never the same for me after he left us in Sicily to attend the Staff College. It was a joy when he rejoined Monty's HQ as a liaison officer before the Normandy landings.

Geoffrey Keating, another captain, was a wartime soldier from the 60th Rifles. He was first in charge of the Eighth Army Film and Photographic Unit. Then he was made head of our public relations department, where he built up Monty as a figurehead and hero of the Eighth Army. Geoffrey travelled all over the desert in his jeep and was often in the front line. He soon became known to all the troops and was always ready for a challenge. He often called in to see Monty, who really valued his contribution to morale. We also greatly enjoyed his visits. This cheerful figure was always ready for a good gossip and invariably had a lively tale to tell.

Last but not least, a vital cog in the big wheel was the commander of the Desert Air Force. Up until the arrival in Tripoli, Air Marshal Sir Arthur 'Mary' Coningham, who had been in charge since the First Army landed in North Africa, held the position, but he was then transferred to Eisenhower's HQ. His successor was Air Vice-Marshal Harry Broadhurst, who had been a fighter pilot in the Battle of Britain.

Harry, who was a wonderful person, was full of enthusiasm and always ready to try new methods to harass the enemy. When Harry took over, the Desert Air Force had won control of the skies. He continued, however, to support the troops on the ground. He got on superbly with Freddie and together they would formulate the role the Air Force would play in battle. The air support that Harry organised was an immense help at the battle of Mareth. The German defences were completely demoralised by wave upon wave of light Hurricane tank-busters, Kitty-bombers and Spitfire squadrons.

The First Crisis

I had only been in the job two days when Monty's Tac HQ had to move to keep in touch with the advancing British Army that had now driven the enemy forces over the Egyptian border into Libya. It was my task to be in charge of the transfer to a given map reference point about 60 miles up the road towards Tobruk. From there we were to turn off into the desert to the HQ's new resting place. Monty went off in the morning with John Poston but was due back at about 5 p.m. By then, the headquarters needed to be set up and ready.

We moved off with me in front in a jeep. There must have been about twenty vehicles in the convoy, but once we got to the coast road we could not lose our way. It was the only route and was nearly straight all the way. We had to go at the same pace as the slowest vehicle, a Sherman tank, whose top speed was about 20 mph. Thinking that was going to be pretty boring, I stopped and told the driver in the vehicle behind that I was going to travel about 30 miles ahead and then wait by the side of the road for the convoy to arrive.

So I buzzed off, and when I reached my destination I sat down to have my haversack lunch and a can of beer, which had no doubt been captured from a German dump. That was a mistake, as I fell asleep in the hot sun. Later I woke up in a terrible quandary, not knowing whether the convoy had gone by. I looked at my watch and realised I must have been there for an hour or so. Help – should I wait and see if the vehicles came along or should I rush off down the road and see if

A desert convoy on the move. (Eton College Library)

Monty examines the coastal defences at Benghazi. (Eton College Library)

I hit the back of the convoy? I chose the latter course of action. After driving at great speed for around ten minutes, thank goodness the convoy appeared in the distance. The first crisis was over.

Daily Routine in the Desert

Monty would be called every morning at seven for breakfast at eight. He said he always used that hour to think about the current situation and

Freddie de Guingand, Monty's brilliant Chief-of-Staff. (Eton College Library)

to decide what was to be done. When Freddie de Guingand stayed the night at Tac HQ, Monty and he always had a discussion after breakfast.

By about 10 o'clock, Monty was ready to visit a divisional HQ and would call on Corps HQ on the way back. Sometimes he would go down to brigade level and, occasionally, even to regimental level. When we learned the identity of the HQ he was to visit and the spot on the map where we would find it, John Poston or I would drive him there. As the desert was so featureless and the troops were moving around so much, our job was not always easy.

Whichever one of us was not with Monty would be sent out to see a divisional commander, or, sometimes, a brigade commander, to find out exactly what was happening in his sector. To start with we found it difficult to communicate with the generals and brigadiers. They did not much like telling us about the situation. But this system of keeping Monty directly in touch was soon accepted and their confidence in us grew.

Monty, after perhaps visiting one of the Corps commanders, would return home at 5 p.m. Then, after being briefed by Bill Williams on the location of the German 15th and 21st Panzer Divisions and the 90th Light Division, we would mark up Monty's map.

This information was invariably correct, thanks in no small part to Enigma, which confirmed the overall picture in North Africa. At the time John and I had no idea of Enigma's existence. Indeed Monty, Bill

Monty talks to the commander of a battalion of the Grenadier Guards in their position near the Mareth Line. (IWM NA1176)

and Freddie were the only ones who knew about the legendary code-breaking machine that helped to win the war by deciphering secret messages from the German High Command. Obviously, it was a tremendous help for them to know what Rommel and Hitler were planning.

Dinner in the mess tent was at 8 p.m., and Monty used this meal as a time for relaxation, producing some subject for discussion. Freddie was a regular guest, and Bill and Brian Robertson often joined us. Also we would sometimes entertain one of the generals from our main HQ, or an outsider.

The Second Crisis

After ten days I went to Monty and said that I believed I ought to return to my regiment, which was in a forward armoured car reconnaissance role, and see some real action. As there was not much going on and our own advance was slowing up, I was bored and had started to miss being among friends of my own age. Monty just said, 'All right, but you'd better come along for the next fortnight while I find someone to replace you.' Two days later I flew back to Cairo with him for the Thanksgiving service for the victory at Alamein. After the service he said, 'You can have the rest of the day and evening off. Meet me at the Guard of Honour at the airstrip at 7 a.m.'

So I shot off to my regiment's HQ in Cairo to see who was there. To my delight I found Robin Brockbank and we went off to the Gezira Sporting Club for lunch. It was already late and we did not finish until 4.00 p.m. So what should we do? Robin, who had always been interested in animals, suggested that we should visit Cairo Zoo.

Monty's trusted ADCs John Poston (left) and the author. (Eton College Library)

We were walking through the elephant house where people were offering the occupants buns. They didn't seem very interested. So Robin took my hat off my head and offered it to an elephant. It shot out its trunk, grabbed the hat and put it in its mouth. Then, it spat out a bit into the front corner of the cage, probably not liking the spiky 12th Lancers badge! I thought I had better try and recover what was left. But, as I was climbing over the bar, the zookeeper luckily grabbed me before I could take on the, by now, extremely irate elephant. So there I was – 6.30 in the evening, no military hat and the shops were shut.

Next morning, after arriving at the airstrip, I waited by the small aeroplane, feeling that I could not attend the Guard of Honour without a hat. Monty arrived, quickly walked down the guard and then came

A Sherman tank travels through the featureless desert sands. (Eton College Library)

The Eighth Army enters Tripoli in triumph. (Eton College Library)

The fabulous parade of the Highland Division. (Eton College Library)

over to the aircraft. 'Johnny, why weren't you at the Guard of Honour as I told you to be?' Remembering that John Poston had specifically told me never to lie, I replied, 'Very sorry, Sir, I haven't got a hat because it was eaten by an elephant yesterday evening.' 'If you feel as bad as that,' he retorted, 'you had better go inside and lie down.'

As we flew back on the half-hour journey, I could not help thinking how my story had gone down. But, as we disembarked, Monty said, 'Are you capable of driving?' (We always drove him.) 'Yes, of course,' I replied. We drove back for about an hour to the Tac HQ, but he never uttered a word, as I soon learnt was his usual procedure. Nothing more was said until dinner that night, when he asked, 'Johnny, what was that extraordinary story you told me about an elephant eating your hat?' So I relayed the strange tale of my missing headgear to the amusement of all at dinner. Having survived that ordeal, I stayed with Monty for another four years. Thanks to the elephant!

Winston Churchill's Visit to Tripoli

We entered Tripoli on 23 January 1943 and Winston and the Chief of the Imperial General Staff (CIGS), General Sir Alan Brooke, made a triumphant visit to celebrate the city's capture ten days later. On the evening before the Prime Minister and the CIGS arrived, John Poston and I decided to make a quick foray to a nightclub in the city after Monty had retired to bed. Unwisely we took Monty's open-topped Humber to drive the 5 miles. This car was the only suitable vehicle to take Monty, Winston and Brooke around the parade area the next day. We came out of the nightclub at about 2.30 a.m. (not having had a particularly good time) to find the car had vanished. We looked at each other in utter dismay.

The immediate plan of action was for John to seek help from the Military Police to find the car. I would stay on the spot in case it was brought back. The Military Police understood our dilemma and everyone available turned out to look for the vehicle. Eventually the car was sighted weaving through the outskirts of Tripoli with a drunken soldier at the wheel. The problem was how to stop it without a crash. Luckily an accident was avoided and the car was returned to us in pristine condition.

Churchill inspects his 'Desert RATs' in Tripoli from Monty's Humber. (IWM E22280)

We returned to our HQ greatly relieved, and, as it was now 4.30 in the morning and getting light, we did not go to bed. Monty never found out anything about the incident.

Monty met Winston and Brooke at the airport in the morning in the open car and, driven by John, they went to the centre of Tripoli for the victory parade. Those who were present will never forget the magnificent turnout of the 51st Highland Division with their pipes and drums. As the Highland Division had fought its way the many miles from Alamein through the dust and horrors of war, their performance was quite remarkable.

That evening Winston wrote a speech that he was going to give to the New Zealand Division the next day. After being asked if the speech could be given to the press, he replied that he would like to see it in print first. So, while he got ready for dinner, he edited it in red ink, and I happened to keep the original.

As usual Monty retired at 9 p.m. with the comment, 'There is a battle to be won, and, if you will forgive me, I am off to bed. These lads will look after you.' We had a memorable time listening to Winston late into the night.

The Arrival of General Leclerc

Around the time of the taking of Tripoli, Monty was told that General Leclerc with a small Free French force had arrived after travelling miles across the desert from Lake Chad. Therefore it was arranged that Monty would meet him on the road outside Tripoli. Leclerc was covered in dust and very excited, but, as he talked very fast in French, we could not translate a word.

Monty turned to me and asked what he was saying. My French was pathetic anyhow, but I thought I had better pretend that I had understood. So I replied, 'The General says he is very pleased to have arrived and wishes to put his force under your command.' Heaven knows what words he had really uttered! Monty then added, 'Tell him I am delighted he has arrived and I am most pleased to have the help of his men.' I had just started translating Monty's words into my appalling French, when, to my delight and relief, Freddie de Guingand, who spoke the language perfectly, arrived and saved my bacon.

Monty shakes hands with General Leclerc. (Eton College Library)

The Flying Fortress

One evening in February when Walter Bedell Smith, Eisenhower's Chief of Staff, came to see Monty at his Tac HQ in Tripoli, the conversation turned to when it was likely that the Eighth Army would reach the important Tunisian city of Sfax. When Monty said that he would get to Sfax by 15 April, Bedell Smith replied that, if Monty got there by that date and before the First Army did, Eisenhower would give him anything he asked for. Monty replied that he would like an aeroplane for his personal use.

The Flying Fortress that Monty demanded from Eisenhower. (Eton College Library)

Monty meets the Flying Fortress crew. (Eton College Library)

Consequently, immediately after the Eighth Army troops entered Sfax, five days early on 10 April, Monty sent a signal to Eisenhower, demanding his aircraft. We understood that Eisenhower did not like the tone of the message, but decided that he must honour his Chief of Staff's undertaking. So this amazing aeroplane, a Flying Fortress (or B-17), soon arrived with an American crew. Monty used her to go back to England for a few days and to travel back and forth to Cairo for the planning of the invasion of Sicily.

A Disturbed Night During the Battle of Mareth

It was well known that the main German defence obstacle in Tunisia on the road from Tripoli was the Mareth Line, a few miles down the coast from Gabes. Its eastern flank rested on the Mediterranean shore and its western side lay in the foothills of the Matmata mountain range. Therefore the Mareth Line, which was only about 25 miles long, was always going to be hard to breach.

As the hilly feature in the west overlooked any attack that might come from the south and the whole approach area was heavily mined and fortified, Monty was ready for a tough battle. The first few days, however, had not gone well for the Eighth Army. The superb 201 Guards' Brigade had taken a terrible mauling while so bravely trying to capture the enemy position in the hills. The 50th Division was also attempting in vain to break through the Wadi Zigzaou, the dry riverbed against the coast.

Eighth Army infantrymen advance across the barren terrain of the desert.
(Eton College Library)

Field Marshal Erwin Rommel, the German commander in North Africa from 1941 to 1943.
(IWM E4062E)

It was the afternoon of 22 March 1943 when Monty sent me to find out how grave the situation was. I came back with a gloomy picture – the defences looked too strong for any likelihood of a breakthrough. Later that night Monty went to bed as usual at 9 p.m. It was 2 a.m. when we were woken up by Oliver Leese, the XXX Corps commander. He told us to rouse Monty as he felt he must see him urgently. Leese was with Monty the best part of an hour. As soon as he left, Monty called us in and said, 'Get Freddie here as soon as possible.'

Freddie de Guingand arrived at 7 a.m. and after about an hour emerged to say that he was going over to the Ops vehicle to arrange a meeting with Brian Horrocks, the X Corps commander, and Bernard Freyberg, the commander of the New Zealand contingent, which was on the left front.

Monty, I believe partly thanks to an idea Freddie suggested at that meeting, now decided to try to gain the initiative with a strong, but narrow, blitz wide on the left flank. Freddie was to set this strategy in

Brian Horrocks, the X Corps commander at Mareth. (Eton College Library)

motion in three days' time. The first objective was to get the Air Force behind the plan. Harry Broadhurst, the air vice-marshal in charge of the Desert Air Force, was full of enthusiasm and said he would bring every available aircraft into action. In fact the aerial part of the plan took a leaf out of the Germans' book and involved attacking the enemy with low-flying aircraft coming out of the late afternoon sun.

The success of the famous left hook at Mareth has been written about over and over again, and I recall the occasion well. Later Monty always mistakenly claimed that these tactics were part of his original plan, but, in fact, they were devised at that meeting in the Ops vehicle on 23 March during the actual battle.

But there was a good reason why his report on Mareth, which was composed some time after the event, was inaccurate in some respects. Up until the capture of Tripoli, Monty would write his diary every night and give it to John Poston or myself to pass to Sergeant Harwood, who would

'Kitty bombers' (Curtiss P-40 Kittyhawks) of the Desert Air Force played havoc with the German defences at Mareth. (Eton College Library)

then type it up. But after Tripoli he started writing it up every three or four days. As a result they were never quite as exact again. Nevertheless, I think listening to his staff and being flexible made him a better general. He was quite prepared to take their ideas on board and change his plans.

The Welcome at Sousse

After the liberation of the Tunisian coastal town of Sousse on 12 April we received a message from the mayor saying that its people would like to give a formal greeting to the Army commander. We asked Monty and he replied that he would be prepared to attend provided the ceremony lasted no longer than half an hour. He suggested that John Poston and I should meet the mayor to see what form the ceremony would take and then make the necessary arrangements.

So off we went the next day and met the mayor, who said that he would like to make a short speech of welcome in the town square where there would be a large gathering. He then added that they had also arranged for a very pretty girl to present a bouquet to Monty. He then rang a bell and along came the girl. The mayor asked us what she should say to Monty. John and I looked at each other, had a quick word and replied that we thought it would be nice if she said, 'Will you kiss me?' So the mayor explained to the girl, who spoke no English, what she should say. Oh dear, she could not get the hang of it at all and kept coming out with words we could not understand. Eventually, however, after lots of rehearsals and laughter, we got a recognisable 'Veel yu keeeze me?' and that seemed good enough.

Monty greets the young lady at Sousse.
(Eton College Library)

26

Two or three days later, we attended a huge local gathering in the main square in Sousse. The mayor stepped forward and made his little speech. Then the girl appeared with the bouquet and, sure enough, she uttered the immortal words, 'Veel yu keeze me?' or something close enough for Monty to understand what he had to do. It was a great success and later Monty asked us if the girl had said the same to us. 'No, no it was reserved for you,' was the answer he received!

The Surrender of Field Marshal Messe

After the enemy forces in North Africa capitulated on 12 May 1943, the Italian Commander-in-Chief, General Messe, surrendered a day later. Messe was then brought to our HQ to see Monty. They sat outside with

Monty chats with the Italian Commander-in-Chief Generale di Armata Messe (seated left), watched by General Kurt Freiherr von Liebenstein (seated right). (Eton College Library)

maps spread out and discussed recent events and the battles they had fought. Monty thoroughly enjoyed himself, and that night Messe even had dinner in the mess with us before he was sent off to his prisoner-of-war camp.

Giovanni Messe's surrender produced a further benefit. Monty was asked if he would like to take over the Italian's luxurious caravan. At the back of the caravan was a bath with its own water tank positioned on the roof. In fact, as the heat in the desert was so intense, the water in the tank was nearly always hot. From then on, Monty used the caravan as his own. He not only took it to Sicily and Italy, but also brought it back to England and used it in the Normandy landings.

A Break in England

Shortly after the capture of Tunis, Monty told John Poston and me that he had decided to go to England for a few days. He needed a break and wanted to see his son, David, who was at school at Winchester.

Monty's fighter escort, a pair of Supermarine Spitfires. (Eton College Library)

Monty gazes out of the Flying Fortress on the trip to England. (Eton College Library)

Monty said that we were to travel with him and that he was also going to take Geoffrey Keating, who had now become the head of our public relations department.

We arrived at Northolt aerodrome on 17 May and were whisked off to stay at Claridge's to the delight of John and myself. We all went to the theatre on the first night, where Monty received a standing ovation. The reception from the public was overwhelming wherever he went. He had not realised how much of a hero and public figure he had become. He enjoyed it to the full.

Monty saw Winston and was received by the King and Queen. He also spent a night with Tom and Phyllis Reynolds (he was the headmaster of David's former preparatory school, Amesbury, near Hindhead, and his guardian while Monty was away). He visited David at Winchester, too.

John and I, however, had a high old time, regularly having champagne sent up to our room and taking our girlfriends to the theatre. On the night before we left, we went down to pay for all the drink we had consumed and for our theatre tickets, only to be told that the General had settled our account completely. What a mistake, but there was nothing to do but to come clean with Monty and tell him that our good livings had been added to his bill in error. But when we owned up Monty looked rather embarrassed and dismissed us, saying, 'No, I wanted you fellows to have a good time.' We left the room, feeling rather deflated. It seemed that there was nobody to thank and show our appreciation to.

King George VI Travels to Tripoli

For security reasons the HQ staff could not be told of the King's forthcoming visit to Tripoli until two days before his arrival on 17 June. Then

Monty and the King in the desert. (IWM HU44165)

Lieutenant-Generals Leese (left) and Lumsden with Monty in North Africa.
(IWM E18416)

there were immediate action stations and everything was painted (heaven knows where they got the paint) in true army fashion. A caravan was prepared for the King with his own thunder box (the army term for a lavatory) set in its own canvas surroundings nearby. On the day after his arrival, the King asked me very quietly if it was possible for him to have a lavatory seat that had not been painted. Oh dear! I immediately visualised the problem.

When the King drove round with Monty, the regiments paraded along the roadsides. The King would stop them and talk to the colonel of each regiment. Later there was a lunch attended by the corps commanders, Leese and Horrocks.

The King was with us for two or three days and each evening after dinner Monty, as was his wont, would go to bed just after 9 p.m. The King certainly enjoyed sitting up with us after Monty had retired and, as the night drew on, he stammered less and less. There was no doubt that he appreciated the relaxed atmosphere of the Tac HQ.

TWO

STORMING SICILY
10 JULY–3 SEPTEMBER 1943

The Eighth Army with the 1st Canadian Division landed on the southeast tip of Sicily and the Seventh US Army further west on 10 July. The Allies met little opposition at first. George Patton's troops quickly took the ports of Licata and Gela and the British forces captured the

British soldiers, their formation badges obscured by the censor, wade ashore during the assault on Sicily. (Eton College Library)

Tanks and their crews wait outside Messina before crossing to Italy.
(Eton College Library)

important town of Syracuse with the minimum of fuss. The Americans then split, with troops under General Patton moving further west, while forces commanded by General Omar Bradley headed north.

Patton took Palermo on 22 July and the Americans then moved east along the northern coast towards the port of Messina. Monty and the Eighth Army, however, met increasingly strong German resistance as they advanced up the eastern side of the island towards Messina. The Allies tried to cut the retreating enemy off, but when Patton reached

Messina on 17 August, huge numbers of German and Italian troops and many vehicles and tanks had already been evacuated across the narrow straits to the Italian mainland.

Algiers, Malta and the Landing in Sicily

Eisenhower had assumed overall command since the landing of the First Army in North Africa and their drive along the coast to Tunis. During the period April to July he was in charge of planning the invasion of Sicily by the Seventh US Army commanded by Patton and the Eighth Army under Monty.

The Americans' planning centre was in Algiers where Eisenhower's High Command was based, but the Eighth Army's was in Cairo. As the

Churchill in North Africa, June 1943. Left to right, standing: *Tedder, Cunningham, Alexander and Monty.* Seated: *Eden, Brooke, Churchill, Marshall and Eisenhower.* (Eton College Library)

Monty and Mountbatten sail from Malta to Sicily. (Eton College Library)

planning centres were in different places, inevitably there were often communication difficulties. But from June onwards Monty let Freddie de Guingand represent him in Cairo as he was very much occupied with the advance from Mareth to Tunis. However, Monty had already been brought into the picture towards the end of April and was extremely disturbed by the plan for the Americans to land in the north-west of Sicily and for the British to land south of Syracuse. He favoured a broad landing in the south with the Americans alongside the British.

When Monty was told to attend a meeting of the High Command in Algiers in early May, he was absolutely determined to get the plan revised. It was therefore necessary to make Eisenhower agree with his way of thinking. Eisenhower, however, was ill and could not attend. So it was essential to make his point to Bedell Smith, his Chief of Staff. It was vital to see him before the meeting and luckily Monty managed to track him down while he was visiting the lavatory. Bedell Smith, according to Monty, immediately concurred. So Monty left Algiers with his plan agreed.

Monty's typist, Sergeant Harwood (centre) at work in the Maltese caves.
(Eton College Library)

Monty did not interfere with the detail of the plan and on 3 July we flew to Malta (his HQ was already set up there in some underground caves). After the invasion plan was finalised, a successful assault on Sicily took place on 10 July. When the beachhead was deep enough, we sailed over three days later with Lord Louis Mountbatten, who came to Malta to cross to Sicily with Monty. Mountbatten was then a commodore and the chief of Combined Operations, a body that gave advice and coordinated the efforts of each armed service during overseas raids on enemy territory.

The Villa Florida at Taormina

One evening our PR officer, Geoffrey Keating, who wandered around the war zone as he liked, sent a wireless message, 'In hotel in Taormina, champagne good, recommend you come here soon.' We passed the message to Monty. Later Monty spoke to Leese, the relevant Corps commander, and gave him the news. Leese was furious that Geoffrey had entered his patch and replied that there was actually heavy fighting on the outskirts of Taormina. Later, for good measure, he decided not to let Geoffrey into his corps area again without personal permission.

When we got to Taormina, which is on the coast road between Catania and Messina, we soon realised that Geoffrey had, in fact, done some excellent reconnaissance. He had found a wonderful house that belonged to a very wealthy Fascist on the edge of a high escarpment

The elegant dining room at the Villa Florida. (Eton College Library)

Geoffrey Keating (right) with Ted Artizone. (IWM HU44173)

with marvellous views of Mount Etna. We moved in and stayed until the landing in Italy. The Villa Florida was fully furnished and contained fabulous glass and china. There was also an Alfa Romeo in the garage, which John Poston and I enjoyed driving. It really was a gorgeous place to be.

The Alfa Romeo left behind by its owner. (Eton College Library)

The Farmyard

After landing in Sicily, we gathered a few chickens together in the hope of producing some eggs. Monty was also presented with a canary. So there were plenty of birds around.

The unpopular peacock. (Eton College Library)

A panorama of Taormina with Mount Etna in the background. (Eton College Library)

I asked Jack Russell, who was in the Royals and was attached to my regiment when we were in Egypt, to come to dinner. The evening was a great success and Monty very much took to Jack and wanted to know all about him. On the evening after the dinner a Jeep drew up at our Tac HQ with a present from Jack. It was a splendid peacock.

Sadly, as you can imagine, our mess staff disliked having to catch the bird each time we moved. So I promised that I would get rid of the peacock before we went over to Italy. When we got to the Villa Florida at Taormina, I launched the poor bird from the top of the 200ft high escarpment. The peacock flapped its wings violently on its flight towards the bottom of the steep hill and soon vanished from view. When we were due to move on, the mess boys were delighted to find that the unfortunate bird was missing.

Monty meets Patton (centre) at Catania. (Eton College Library)

Monty's Meeting in Sicily with General Patton

Monty had encountered General Patton when he came to the Tac HQ once or twice during the advance from Tripoli to Tunis. He immediately took to the American general and liked his easy-going forthcoming character. They met again at Catania when the fighting in Sicily was over. After Monty and Patton had greeted each other in the usual friendly manner, the party sat down. Monty, however, remained standing. He was clearly in command.

The first item on the agenda was what was known as fraternisation – in this case the problem was how far soldiers could go when they were talking to Italian girls. George Patton quickly came to the point. 'I say fraternisation ain't fornication – that is if you keep your hat on and the weight on your elbows.' His comment caused much laughter. Monty joined in but he did not much like the attention shifting towards Patton. The rest of the meeting took place in an altogether cooler atmosphere.

The Demise of the Flying Fortress

One day Monty sent a signal to Patton asking if he could land the Flying Fortress at Palermo airport and come to see him. Patton agreed and so Monty, Freddie de Guingand, Harry Broadhurst and I went to Catania airport to fly to Palermo.

As was the custom, I sat at the front in the glass nose of the plane below the pilots' seats, where the bomb aimer would normally be. As we landed at Palermo, it became obvious that our American pilot had not checked the length of the runway. The ground loomed up and there seemed to be no chance of stopping before the hangars. But, just as the end seemed nigh, the pilot jammed on all the brakes on one side of the aircraft. The plane then miraculously swung round and collapsed on its side. A quick exit was achieved. Monty was quite unperturbed, but it was the end of the poor Flying Fortress, which had proved so useful. Her replacement was a Dakota.

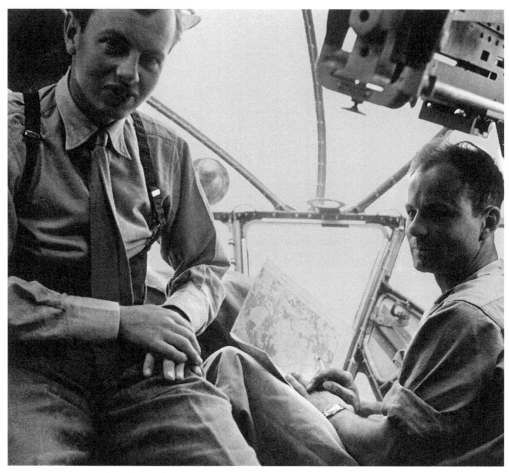

The author (left) in his usual position in the nose of the Flying Fortress.
(Eton College Library)

Cigarettes

Towards the end of our time in North Africa, and thereafter, Monty was sent large consignments of cigarettes to hand out to the troops. So whenever we went out in the car, we took plenty of packets for Monty to distribute. If he stopped on the roadside to talk to the soldiers or met them at divisional or regimental HQ, he would always say, 'I think you might like some of these. I don't use them myself, you know.' Then he would tell the soldiers what was going on. It was a huge morale booster for the men.

Later, in Normandy, I remember Monty asking me to deliver 90,000 cigarettes each, which he had bought out of his personal Comfort Fund money, to 49th and 50th Divisions. Monty's generosity certainly paid a big dividend, as the soldiers were absolutely delighted to receive these unexpected gifts from their commanding officer.

Monty distributes cigarettes to his men. (Eton College Library)

THREE

ASSAULT ON ITALY
3 SEPTEMBER–31 DECEMBER 1943

The Eighth Army under Monty crossed the short distance from Sicily to Reggio on Italy's toe on 3 September, and encountered little resistance. Later that day, British ships also landed a parachute division at the large and strategically important port of Taranto, further east on the heel of Italy.

A flotilla carries Eighth Army troops from Sicily to Italy. (Eton College Library)

But, when the Fifth US Army arrived at Salerno, south of Naples on the western coast, six days later, General Mark Clark's men faced heavy German shelling and bombardment. Consequently the Commander-in-Chief, Alexander, ordered the Eighth Army to travel nearly 300 miles to threaten the enemy forces, which were confronting the Americans. The leading troops of the Eighth Army and the right flank of the United States forces met on 16 September.

Soon after the Salerno beachhead was secured on 20 September, Monty was told to transfer operations to Italy's Adriatic coast and begin a movement northwards towards Rome. Clark captured Naples and Monty took Foggia and its vital airfields on 1 October. But, after fierce fighting along the Rivers Trigno and Sangro, the weather closed in. Indeed, the whole area around the Sangro was waterlogged by 9 November and no army vehicles could move off road due to the appalling mud. The Eighth Army had made no further progress and the Adriatic coast was in the firm grip of winter when Monty heard, on Christmas Eve, that he was to be recalled to England to take command of all the land forces that would be involved in the Second Front.

The heavy artillery barrage at night over the Straits of Messina. (Eton College Library)

The Landing in Italy

Left to right: the author, Harvey Butcher (Ike's naval aide), Monty and Eisenhower on the jetty at Messina. (Eton College Library)

On the night of 3 September there was a heavy barrage as our troops crossed the narrow Straits of Messina from Sicily to Italy. As Eisenhower and Monty watched the action from the harbour jetty at Messina, they did not know what opposition they were likely to meet, but they had heard that the Italians were possibly ready to surrender. They had no idea, however, what the Germans would do.

When our forces had completed the crossing, they found that the Italians had put up notices saying, 'Welcome to the British'. But the trouble was that the toe of Italy, Calabria, was hilly and marvellous

A big Italian welcome. (Eton College Library)

defensive country. The Italian people seemed to be pleased to see us, but it was immediately clear that the Allied advance would not be easy.

The Bailey Bridge

We soon discovered that the Germans had blown holes in most of the roads. Therefore a Bailey bridge was required to make most Italian towns and villages accessible for vehicles. The Bailey bridge was the most marvellous invention and we would have made no progress in Italy without it. They came in prefabricated bits, similar to the old Meccano sets, and the engineers just used to join the parts together. If, however, a river needed to be crossed, they usually placed the bits of the bridge on pontoons.

The longest Bailey bridge extended to 1,200ft across the River Sangro, which meets the sea between Pescara and Vasto on central

The long Bailey bridge over the Sangro. (Eton College Library)

An Italian bridge blown up by the Germans. (Eton College Library)

Italy's Adriatic coast. It was a truly magnificent piece of engineering. The problem for the constructors at the Sangro was that the pillars of the old bridge were still there and needed to be used. If the engineers had not calculated their angles exactly, the sections of the Bailey bridge would have missed the pillars and disappeared into the deep water below.

Alexander's Visit

On 5 September General Sir Harold Alexander, our commander-in-chief, flew into the airfield at Reggio, which had been cleared recently. Alex had come to tell Monty that the Italians had just signed a complete surrender but that it was not going to be announced until 8 September. He continued that the Italian Army was ready to seize Rome and the ports of Taranto, Naples and Bari.

The commander-in-chief, Alexander, Monty and Bedell Smith (Ike's Chief-of-Staff).
(Eton College Library)

Alex was full of these plans, but Monty warned him that this scenario might not occur. Monty told him that the Germans would disarm the Italians immediately they found out about the surrender and that the Italians did not have enough fight left in them anyhow. Monty was proved right on both counts. That is exactly what happened.

A Goose for Dinner

One autumn day, when we were driving up to the front line, we came upon a farmyard which had been heavily shelled and whose occupants had fled. Five geese, however, had remained. When Monty saw the birds, he said, 'Johnny, get one of those for dinner.' But I had no idea how to secure our supper. I had a pistol, but I was not much good with that. So

The author (left) and Monty take a drive during the Italian campaign.
(Eton College Library)

I looked around and spotted the spade that we always carried on cars in case they got stuck in the desert.

I approached the smallest goose with my improvised weapon and gave it a clip round the head. The blow did the bird no harm at all. It just spread its wings and charged me. I gave it another bash with the spade. No good again. Eventually I somehow managed to wrestle the unfortunate goose to the ground and administer the *coup de grâce*. It was not a great effort on my part. But Monty had thoroughly enjoyed the farce and we had a delicious dinner later.

A Bath in Wine

After crossing from Sicily to southern Italy, we found that our living conditions became extremely primitive. Monty's Tac HQ was often

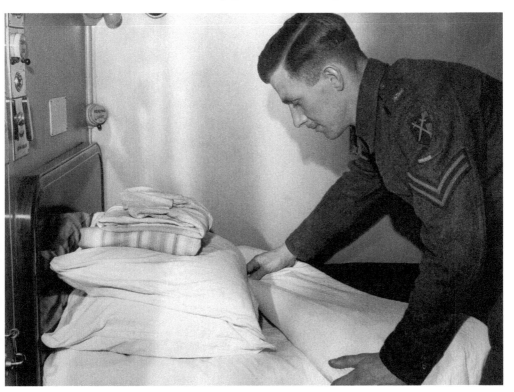

Corporal English, Monty's loyal batman. (Eton College Library)

billeted in some house or other that invariably had no running water. So Monty's soldier servant, Corporal English, had to take heated water in a receptacle, known as a jerry can, to the bath.

One evening I was walking down the passage of a run-down cottage that we had occupied near Bari when Monty shouted from the bathroom, 'Get Corporal English to bring some cold water.' There was a jerry can filled with what I presumed was water, standing in the passage outside the bathroom. So I opened the door and found Monty in the bath shaking his feet up and down. 'The bath is far too hot,' he cried. So I handed him the can and he started to pour the contents into the bath. The liquid, which unfortunately turned out to be Marsala wine, hit him just above the knees. 'You bloody fool!' he yelled.

Military Appointments and Postings

Monty always wanted to know what postings were being made. He took great interest and made many appointments personally from corps

The author attends to some office work. (Eton College Library)

commanders down to colonels of regiments. He always followed his protégés' later careers with interest and often helped them climb further up the Army's promotion ladder. If he did not know a prospective appointee, he would ask about his military service record, age, experience of fighting in the front line and history. In short, he wanted to know everything about each officer under his command.

On the advance through Italy, Monty was once informed of a mutiny of fighting soldiers who had been wounded. When they returned to the front, these men, to their horror, discovered that they were not being posted back to the regiments with whom they had previously fought. Monty was absolutely furious when he heard these reports and said, 'Get the military secretary responsible for these postings here at once.' When Colonel Coghill arrived, Monty gave him the most terrible rocket. 'These fellows are right,' he pointed out vehemently, 'the British Army is based on its regimental history.'

A Leg Pull Too Far

As December drew on, the buzz was that Monty or Alex would soon be going back to England to prepare for and to command the invasion of Europe. Whenever we met Alex's personal staff, the conversation would invariably turn to who it would be. Each side would exclaim, 'I hope it is our fellow.'

One day, we received a signal from Alex's PA, Bill Cunningham, asking if Monty would like Alex's caravans. 'Oh lord,' we said, 'that means that Alex

A British patrol advances cautiously through the rubble of bombed buildings in Italy. (IWM NA8440)

has got the job.' There was great gloom in our camp that night and nothing more was heard until the next day when Freddie de Guingand came up to Tac HQ. Monty asked Freddie if he had heard anything, and, on being told 'No', said, 'I think you had better fly back to see Alex and find out if I am taking over from him out here.'

So Freddie flew back and asked Alex the vital question. To his great surprise, Alex replied that he had never heard of any such plans. Freddie then telephoned me and asked who had sent the original signal, as Alex knew nothing about it. When I told him that it was Bill Cunningham, Alex quickly contacted his PA to ask if this was true. 'Oh yes,' said Bill, 'it was just a leg pull on Monty's lads.'

Alex thought it was very funny. Monty, however, was not amused but was greatly relieved. Nothing more was said about the prank.

Sleeping in the Caravan

Once, when I had not gone out with Monty in the afternoon, I decided to have a lie-down in his caravan, which was much more

The author sleeps peacefully in Monty's caravan. (Eton College Library)

comfortable than my camp bed, and read a book. A fellow officer came over to seen me and found that I was fast asleep. He retreated, grabbed his camera, took a photograph of me in a blissful slumber, and then, luckily, woke me up. It was just as well that he roused me. Monty was due back soon.

Farewell to the Eighth Army

It was Christmas Eve 1943 when we finally heard that Monty, rather than Alex, had been selected to return to England to command the landing in Europe. There was, of course, great rejoicing in Monty's mess that night, but also concern about our futures. Would we be going with the new commander-in-chief of the 21st Army Group, or back to our regiments?

It was not long before Monty told Noel Chavasse, a fellow ADC, and me that we would accompany him. Freddie de Guingand, Bill Williams and Miles Graham, who had replaced Brian Robertson as his Q, would follow too. We also learnt that we would be allowed to take our soldier servants. This was great news, as, by now, mine, Charlie Saunders, was a friend and support.

When we heard that Monty was leaving, the first task was to organise a farewell gathering of the Eighth Army, which was to include all officers down to colonels of regiments. A strong representation from the Air Force was also due to attend. Freddie chose the old theatre in Vasto, where our Main HQ was based, for this auspicious occasion on 30 December.

Monty told me to compose a brief farewell speech. He certainly hacked about what I had written, but it turned out to be an emotional goodbye. Before he spoke, Monty was unduly quiet and we could all see how moved he was. He was escorted to the stage by Freddie and started by apologising if his voice should let him down. He then said that we would all understand how he felt about leaving the Eighth Army, which meant so much to him and had served him so well. That certainly brought a lump to all our throats.

He ended by reading a personal message to all the troops. There was tremendous cheering and clapping when he left the stage with tears in

Monty says goodbye to his Eighth Army commanders. Left to right: *de Guingand, Broadhurst, Monty, Freyberg, Allfrey and Dempsey.* (Eton College Library)

his eyes. Later he recovered his composure to pose for a photograph with those members of his staff who were most closely associated with his Eighth Army victories.

The Return to England

It was 31 December when we set off from an airstrip next to the Sangro for Marrakech, where Monty was to meet Winston, who was

convalescing there after a recent stroke. We stayed in the Mamounia Hotel, which seemed luxurious compared to our state of accommodation as we moved up Italy. The next morning, on New Year's Day, Monty said that he thought it was a good idea that I should go back to England straight away to find out where our HQ would be and whether accommodation had been arranged nearby. If not, he suggested that I book some rooms or a hotel.

An aeroplane was arranged to fly me back to Northolt immediately. When I arrived in England, I went straight to the War Office to be told that the planning of 'Overlord' (the code name for the Normandy landings) was to take place at St Paul's School in West Kensington, where Monty had been educated. Also, I was informed that arrangements were being made for Monty to have a flat close by in Latymer Court, just across the main road to Hammersmith.

A Sherman tank speeds through the Italian countryside during the winter of 1943.
(Eton College Library)

However, we needed alternative living quarters until the flat became vacant and was refurbished. So, which hotel should I book? The decision was not difficult. We had stayed at Claridge's for three nights after reaching Tripoli and enjoyed ourselves immensely. We had six glorious weeks there until the flat was ready. Monty certainly appreciated the extremely comfortable surroundings. He had a large bedroom with a sitting room on the first floor. Noel and I shared a bedroom on the other side of the sitting room. Claridge's was a mighty good army billet!

FOUR

PLANNING FOR 'OVERLORD'
JANUARY–JUNE 1944

Most of Monty's time in the first half of 1944 was spent planning and preparing for D-Day and the forthcoming invasion of France. Eisenhower, the Supreme Commander; Tedder, Ike's deputy; Ramsay, the Naval Commander-in-Chief; Leigh-Mallory, the Air Commander-in-Chief; Coningham, the head of Tactical Air Forces; Bedell Smith, Ike's Chief of Staff; and Monty, the Army Commander-in-Chief, were the men in charge of the top secret initiative, known as Operation 'Overlord', whose objective was to land Dempsey's Second British Army and Bradley's First American Army on five Normandy beaches, west of the River Orne. Heavy aerial bombardment of all German military installations and communication systems along the northern French coast was to precede the invasion.

Monty and his colleagues had many meetings, first, at Overlord's planning HQ at St Paul's School in West London and, later, at Southwick House, near Portsmouth, to ensure that the complicated logistics of an operation, designed to deliver over 150,000 soldiers from more than 2,000 ships onto the Normandy coast on D-Day, did not fail. They knew full well that successful assaults on the beaches (code-named Sword, Juno, Gold, Omaha and Utah) would provide a vital footing in

Normandy, which would be the catalyst for the liberation of German-occupied France.

Where and When – Preparing for D-Day

On 2 January I went down to Northolt airfield to meet Monty on his return to England from Marrakech. He had just sat down in the car when he asked me where we were going. I explained that I had booked

A planning room at St Paul's School. (IWM HU44418)

rooms at Claridge's as the Latymer Court flat was not yet ready. 'That is fine' he said.

As I have said before, life in the hotel was superb, and I remember we had dinner at 8 o'clock in the restaurant at the table immediately to the right of the entrance every night. Monty went to bed at nine, the same time as he retired in the desert. Breakfast was at eight, as we always had to be at 21st Army Group Planning HQ at St Paul's by nine.

It must have been 3 or 4 January when Monty informed us that 1 May was the proposed date for the landing in Normandy and added, straight away, that we were to tell no one. His policy was that it was much better

Monty at his desk. (Eton College Library)

for those close to him to know the date and also much safer, as it stopped them guessing.

The early days at St Paul's were taken up with briefings on the plans that had been made for the landing of British, American and Canadian forces in France, when Monty's predecessor, General Paget, was in command. But Monty also wanted to make some changes to the HQ staff, so one of the first things he did at St Paul's was to get hold of the military secretary, Brigadier Gannon, to draw up a list of potential recruits.

It must have been frustrating for Jack Gannon, when Monty dismissed most of Paget's staff and a good many of the new candidates with an abrupt 'Too old, too old.' It seemed that he was most reluctant to retain or appoint anybody over forty. As usual Monty wanted a young team round him.

Dealing with the Press

Monty believed that communications with the press should be of the highest order and insisted that war correspondents were given good guidance and background talks. It was usually Freddie de Guingand's job to brief the gentlemen of the press and he often had to prevent sensitive and even secret information about, for example, forthcoming battles, appearing in the newspapers.

Freddie's preferred method of stopping a story going to print was to summon the committee of accredited war correspondents, which they themselves had elected. He would then be totally frank with its members, tell them as much of the truth as he dared, and point out that it was up to them to ensure that the item in question did not appear in their or any of the other papers.

Taking the journalists into his confidence and creating a mutual bond of trust certainly worked. Alan Moorehead and Paul Holt of the *Daily Express*, the *Daily Telegraph*'s Christopher Buckley and the *Daily Mail*'s Alexander Clifford, who were all good friends of Freddie, always ensured that their colleagues did not rock the boat by running an unauthorised scoop.

The Betting Book

We used to make odd bets when we were with the Eighth Army and Monty used to record the wagers on scraps of paper. But, when we came back to England and were living in Latymer Court, Monty started entering all the bets in a little black book, usually with a signature attached. Nearly all the wagers were for £5, which was a fair sum in those days. Monty never proposed a bet, but was quite ready to accept one. He liked winning and would immediately write to the loser requesting payment.

Monty did particularly well with bets concerning the date of the end of the war with Germany. For instance, Freddie de Guingand struck several such bets with Monty in North Africa on 4 March 1943, which are listed below:

1 January 1944	Even £5
1 April 1944	Even £5
1 February 1945	£15 to £5
25 March 1945	£5 to £10.

In Italy, Eisenhower also bet Monty an even fiver that the war would be over by Christmas 1944.

Monty also won quite a lot of money on bets struck at our 21st Army Group HQ. In January 1944, Admiral Ramsay bet Monty an even £5 that the war would be over by 1 January 1945, and in June 1944 the Canadian commander, General Crerar, bet him another even fiver that it would end by 1 September 1944.

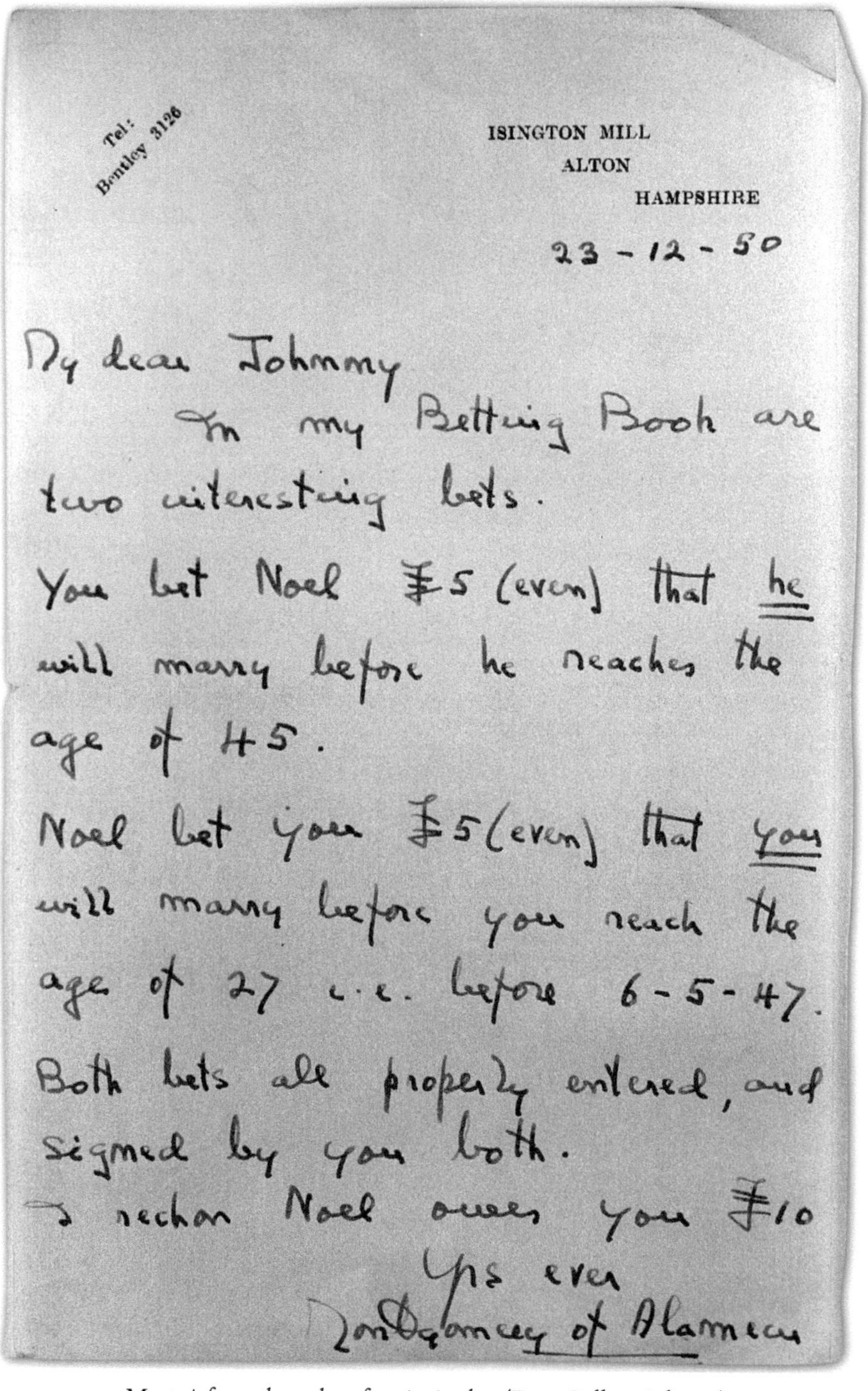

Tel:
Bentley 3126

ISINGTON MILL
ALTON
HAMPSHIRE

23 - 12 - 50

My dear Johnny,

In my Betting Book are two interesting bets.

You bet Noel £5 (even) that <u>he</u> will marry before he reaches the age of 45.

Noel bet you £5 (even) that <u>you</u> will marry before you reach the age of 27 i.e. before 6 - 5 - 47.

Both bets are properly entered, and signed by you both.

I reckon Noel owes you £10

Yrs ever
Montgomery of Alamein

Monty informs the author of a winning bet. (Eton College Library)

Harry Crerar (second left with cigarette) lost his bet with Monty. (IWM B9473)

On 1 June 1944, General Patton bet Monty £100 that the British armed forces would be involved in another war in Europe within ten years of the end of the current hostilities. Patton also made a more eccentric wager, when he bet an even £10 that the first Grand National run after the war would be won by an American-owned horse.

There were also entries of a more trivial nature. For example, my fellow ADC, Noel Chavasse, and I struck a wager on the dates of our respective marriages. Years later I received a letter from Monty, dated 23 December 1950 (the day after the bet fell due), informing me that he reckoned Noel owed me £10!

D-Day Delay

In late January Monty said, 'Get on to the Prime Minister's office and tell them I want to see him urgently.' Eventually the answer came back that Winston would see him at 10 p.m. When I gave Monty the message, he retorted, 'That is ridiculous. He knows perfectly well that I will be in bed at that time. Telephone the officer in charge again and I will speak to him myself.' So I rang back and, sure enough, Monty got the appointment changed to six in the evening.

When we arrived, Monty immediately told Winston that he wanted to postpone D-Day for a month to enable additional landing craft to be transported back from Italy. Winston replied that it could not be done. He explained that he had promised Stalin that the invasion would be on 1 May to take the pressure off the Russian Front. 'If you put it back by a month,' Monty said, 'I will guarantee you success. If you don't, I cannot.'

In fact the proposed date for D-Day was soon changed to 5 June.

The portrait by Augustus John that Monty did not like. ((IWM HU44414)

Sitting for Augustus John

In February Monty began sittings for a portrait by Augustus John. He wanted his son, David, to have a painting of his father in case he did not survive the war. Kit Dawnay, Monty's recently appointed military assistant, negotiated the fee with the artist on the chief's behalf. I remember Monty was delighted when Kit managed to reduce the cost of the commission from £500 to £400. In the end Monty did not buy the portrait as he thought it did not represent a true likeness. John eventually sold the picture to the University of Glasgow, but Monty was not alone in believing that it was not the charismatic painter's greatest work.

George Bernard Shaw, who met and talked with Monty in John's London studio in Tite Street, later wrote to the veteran artist, criticising the portrait. The great playwright complained that the subject did not look the viewer straight in the eye, as Monty always did. He also pointed out that John's image filled the canvas, suggesting a large, tall man, which Monty definitely was not.

On another occasion, when I went with Monty to a sitting, we passed a very attractive girl coming down the steep staircase from the studio. It was the famous actress Vivien Leigh, whom John was also painting at the time. As we entered the studio, we caught the artist wiping a canvas with an oily rag. Closer examination revealed that he had erased all his recent painting of the actress, except for her beautiful head and neck and her elegant legs. Nothing in between remained. I have always believed that the voluptuous old boy so enjoyed painting Miss Leigh's magnificent torso that he wanted her to pose again and again!

Visiting the Troops on Rapier

At the beginning of May I set forth with Monty on a special train, called Rapier, to tour England, Scotland and Wales for a fortnight. The purpose of our trip was to visit every formation that was to take part in Overlord. Kit Dawnay, Corporal English (Monty's soldier servant), two chefs, two drivers with two cars, and two wonderful ladies (the manager of the train and a typist) travelled with us.

Rapier's destination is checked with the train's driver. (Eton College Library)

The procedure was much the same each day. As soon as we pulled up at a station, the cars were unloaded, a man plugged in the telephone and the relevant corps commander was there to meet us. The night before, Monty had been given a detailed itinerary, which included our destination, the time of our visit, which troops we were meeting and the name of their commander. The organisation and attention to detail was absolutely amazing.

After meeting the corps commanders, Monty took off to see the regiments. He liked to see as many troops as possible. He would walk down the ranks and ask them to stand at ease so that he could talk to them. This exercise took about half an hour and then he would ask the troops to gather round. He would stand on a jeep and tell them as much as he

Sergeant Gouk serves lunch to Monty on Rapier. (Eton College Library)

dared about the progress of the war and what was going to happen in the future.

On one occasion we were due to visit a Guards' armoured division at Bridlington in Yorkshire. As he had an idea he was not popular with the Guards, Monty was quite apprehensive. Things could not have gone worse at the beginning. We were two hours late and they had been standing there for a long time. As Monty walked down the line, he told the sergeant-major that he wanted the troops to stand at ease. He replied that they were standing at ease! Monty really wanted to chat with the soldiers, but whenever he asked them a question, they just replied, 'Sir'.

Monty addresses troops from his Jeep before the invasion of Europe. (Eton College Library)

It took a long time and a lot of explaining, but in the end, they began to understand that he wanted them to be less formal.

On another day we visited an artillery brigade near Battle in Sussex. Later, at lunch, Monty said to the corps commander, General Ritchie, 'Who was that old fellow who commanded that brigade?' The general replied that his name was Hugh Crosland. 'As a matter of fact he happens to be one of my trustees,' I pointed out. 'That doesn't make him any good,' Monty retorted.

Churchill in his favourite siren suit with Monty, shortly before the Normandy landings. (Eton College Library)

The Prime Minister Dines at Broomfield House

On the afternoon of 20 May, three weeks after we had moved our HQ from London to Portsmouth to be close to the launching point of the invasion, Monty took Winston to inspect the local marshalling yards and supply areas that housed all the paraphernalia our forces would need when they reached Normandy. The Prime Minister stayed for dinner in Monty's mess at Broomfield House and then returned to his train to travel back to London.

During a discussion on the horrors of politics at dinner, Winston, who was in his usual sparkling form, made a memorable remark – 'There is one advantage being in politics. If you are sacked, you can call your opponent a bloody liar and your sacking a disgrace and move over to the other side. But, if you are in the army, you must take your sacking with a "Yes, Sir" and, when in church, you must even say that it was an act of God!'

How I envied Winston's gift of being able to come up with a *bon mot* on every occasion.

Monty's Double

A few days before D-Day a plan was devised that a man dressed as Monty should visit the troops in the South of France, calling at Gibraltar on the

Monty obtains some fishing tips on the Spey. (Eton College Library)

Monty with an admiring crowd at Dalwhinnie station. (Eton College Library)

Monty picnics on his Scottish trip. Left to right: *Dick Carver, Gerry Feilden and Kit Dawnay.* (Eton College Library)

way. The idea was that the impersonator's presence in Gibraltar would be reported back to Germany by their spy network and that their top brass would then feel that there were unlikely to be any immediate landings on the French coast.

Monty's double was Clifton James, an Australian-born actor from Birmingham, who was serving in the Royal Army Pay Corps. From a distance he looked sufficiently similar to play the part adequately. When this fellow arrived at HQ, he was put in sergeant's battle dress. Apart from Monty, we were the only ones to know his real identity. The first problem occurred when he passed the camp commandant without saluting and was given an almighty rocket. So we decided it was safer to dress him as an officer.

Monty's impersonator even came with us on a Scottish trip. Freddie de Guingand, Kit Dawnay and I took Monty to Dalwhinnie so that he could disappear and have three days' rest before D-Day. I recall that the train parked in the station next to the distillery and that we went fishing on the Spey one day. We also visited the nearby home of Gerry Feilden, who was number two at our Q department. Monty's double, however, had to leave early to prepare for his mission.

On 30 May James set off for Gibraltar, dressed as Monty and covered in medals. I even had to lend my hat to the man playing his ADC. This strange ploy must have worked. A message was later received on an open line, which had previously been used by a captured German agent, confirming that Monty was not in England at the time.

The double once asked if he could receive Monty's pay for the period he was standing in for him. When told what it was, James replied that he would rather have his own wages! If I remember rightly, Monty's pay was a meagre £9 per day.

The Missing Letters

Just before D-Day, Monty sent his small group of liaison officers around the country to make final contact with the various divisional commanders whose troops were due to take part in the Normandy landings. They hurried to complete the allotted tasks so that they could then scoot off to London and elsewhere to spend a little time with their wives or girlfriends. Wishing to make the most of the last short break they would have for some time, the LOs also arranged to meet up for a celebratory drink in a hotel in Brighton before they went back to Monty's HQ at Portsmouth.

When the LOs finally left the hotel's bar in, shall we say, a happier frame of mind, John Poston discovered that his jeep had been stolen. John's colleagues were most amused to learn that he was not at all worried about the theft of the army vehicle, but was absolutely distraught at the thought of the opportunistic burglar reading the pile of love letters he had left on the passenger seat from his girlfriend, Audrey Surtees, who was a cousin of mine.

Monty inspects a glider in an outsized pair of white fur gauntlets. (Eton College Library)

The Cover Plan

Much of the time at our HQ at Southwick House, near Portsmouth, and, indeed, before at St Paul's School, was taken up with a secret initiative known as the Cover Plan. As there was enormous activity in the ports along the Channel coast in the first five months of 1944, the enemy obviously had a good idea that an assault on the continent was imminent. So the Cover Plan's main objective was to persuade the Germans that the main landings in France would take place around Cap Gris Nez in the Calais area rather than on the Normandy beaches.

We had various means of deceiving the enemy into thinking that the Pas-de-Calais was where Operation Overlord would take place. The Air Force obviously hit the German defences in Normandy hard during the pre-D-Day period, but a lot of effort was also spent bombing targets in the Calais area to suggest that the Allies were softening up that locality for the eventual landing.

In addition, many other steps were taken to make the Germans think that a group of armies was congregating in Kent. A mock HQ was even set up in Dover and all radio messages to and from the genuine one in Southwick House were sent there by landline. Numerous fake landing craft were positioned in ports all along the south-east coast, and Canadian and American troops were relocated to the Folkestone-Dover area to perform exercises, such as embarkation.

After D-Day, however, the Cover Plan was to assume a further dimension. When the Normandy landings had taken place, we hoped that the German commander, Rommel, would believe that they were merely distractive manoeuvres, designed to draw many of his troops away from the vicinity of Calais, Belgium and Holland, thus making the main Allied attack around Cap Gris Nez easier. This scheme was also supposed to convince the enemy that the main invasion of France would not be launched until some time after D-Day.

An entry in my diary, written in Normandy, for 10 July, over a month after D-Day, reveals that the Cover Plan was amazingly still having the desired effect.

'There is no doubt that the enemy have completely bought our cover plan. They are convinced that we intend to land General Patton's army north of the Seine. They are therefore keeping a large number of troops in that area – just as we want, for we do not wish to see any more divisions opposite us here. They cannot understand why we are bombing down all the bridges over the Seine if we are going to land more troops to the south and not to the north of it. Long may they think so.'

Soldiers play chess during the long wait before D-Day. (Eton College Library)

The Long Wait

If the commanders were getting frustrated waiting for D-Day, so were the officers and their men. Indeed, there is evidence to suggest that the Normandy landings would not have been postponed any longer. As the troops had been cooped up on the ships for some days and were absolutely raring to go to France, Monty and Eisenhower were certain that morale would be seriously affected if the Supreme Commander announced a further delay. As everybody had been briefed, they also knew that it would be difficult to ensure security if the men were taken off the boats. That is why I believe that Ike would have given the order to go, even if the weather forecast for 6 June had not been favourable

The invasion leaders. Left to right: *Bradley, Ramsay, Tedder, Eisenhower, Monty, Leigh–Mallory and Bedell Smith.* (IWM CH12109)

The Decision to Go

All the planning had been geared for D-Day to be on 5 June. There were only three days when the tide was right for the Normandy landings. A low tide in the very early morning was needed to deal with the defence obstacles and a higher tide was required later to enable the landing craft to get as far up the beaches as possible. So, 5 June represented the best option, 6 June the next best, and 7 June was also a possible. After that, however, the tides were too unfavourable and then the landings would have to be postponed for a fortnight.

The weather forecast had been closely watched for a week. But, as the preferred day grew closer, the tension rose dramatically. The trouble was that the weather picture indicated a far from settled period.

I am indebted to Monty's memoirs for the timing of the events of the next few days at Southwick House. On 3 June the forecast was bad with a heavy depression due to spread south. This meant that the prospect of suitable weather on the night of 4 June and the morning of 5 June was not looking good. Monty was for going and Eisenhower agreed to activate the plan at a conference at 9.30 p.m. on 3 June. But it was also stipulated that the final

Monty and Ike take a walk. (US National Archives)

decision to go would need to be taken early on 4 June, even though some of the convoys would have already set sail.

When we met again at Southwick House at 4 a.m., the weather reports were bad. Ramsay for the Navy reckoned it would be possible to land but did not much like the idea. Tedder, however, was for postponement. The Deputy Supreme Commander argued convincingly that his air support plans could not be carried out and control of the skies could not be guaranteed. Eisenhower quickly summed up the situation and put off the initiative until 6 June.

Another meeting was then held on the evening of 4 June where they agreed to reconvene at 4 a.m. the next day. The Met Office experts said the storm in the Channel was slackening and predicted calmer conditions for the days thereafter. On hearing that the weather was set fair, within a few minutes Eisenhower said, 'Yes, we go.'

I can still recall the heavy feeling of apprehension as we left the room early on that dark and windy summer morning of 5 June.

FIVE

THE BATTLE OF NORMANDY

6 JUNE–19 AUGUST 1944

Although the Americans initially experienced problems scaling the steeps cliffs above Omaha beach and suffered heavy casualties, D-Day was an unqualified success and a tactical surprise to the Germans. The Allies quickly gained ground and were 6 miles inland by the next day

British troops come ashore on Sword Beach, 6 June 1944. (IWM B5114)

(D-Day +1). By D-Day + 4 (10 June), the invading armies firmly held a line across Normandy, 60 miles long and between 8 and 12 miles deep.

Monty's master plan for the land battle in Normandy was to draw the main enemy strength gradually towards the British forces on the eastern flank and eventually use the Americans to break out in the west. It is well

Sherman tanks and their crews packed onto a tank landing craft on D-Day.
(IWM A23671)

known that this strategy took some time to come to fruition. The Allies did not capture Caen until 10 July and did not clear its eastern suburbs until 20 July. Moreover, there was speculation in late July and early August that Eisenhower and Churchill were about to relieve Monty of his command, as Allied progress was too slow. It was even claimed that the British troops were leaving all the fighting to the Americans.

Monty's critics, however, soon had to eat their words. The Allies eventually trapped the Germans south of Caen, in the locality known as the 'Falaise Pocket'. They inflicted huge numbers of casualties on the enemy, took many prisoners and destroyed large amounts of military equipment. The surviving German forces, realising the game was up, retreated rapidly and the Battle of Normandy was effectively over by 19 August.

D-Day

The following is the entry in my diary for 6 June 1944, one of the most famous dates in the history of warfare.

'D-Day had arrived. I got up at 0630 and went down to Southwick House to find out the form. The airborne landings at 0100 hours had gone exceptionally smoothly. Only 30 of the 1,300 planes carrying parachutists and towing gliders had failed to return to base. 6th Airborne Division had already reported that it was in the correct position. As yet there had been no enemy reaction in the air or on the sea. Although a few small craft had capsized owing to the rough seas, a mine had sunk only one LCT. The weather appeared to be clouding over, but the heavy bombers had managed to bomb German gun emplacements

A Sherman Firefly tank comes ashore from a tank landing ship. (IWM B5130)

0730 hours was zero hour for the United States Army to touch shore. There was still no news of the Americans by 1000 hours, but the five British Army brigades were known to have got ashore successfully. German radio had announced at 0730 hours that the invasion of the continent had started and that parachutists had landed at the mouth of the Seine. It therefore seemed that these dummy parachutes had been successful, as a number of those equipped with banging gadgets had been dropped in that area.

No news of the American landings came through until 1530, when a flash was sighted, saying that the beaches were clear of the enemy. Meanwhile, I Corps and XXX Corps of the Second British Army were pushing inland. They had made about four miles and were now just three miles short of Caen. At 1800 hours we heard that our 21st Army Group

Tac HQ and my fellow ADC, Noel Chavasse, had not yet landed, but the C-in-C was still determined to cross the Channel. We therefore boarded the destroyer, HMS *Faulknor*, at 2200 hours. At 2215 we set sail for France.'

D-Day+1

I went up onto HMS *Faulknor*'s deck at 0530 hours on 7 June, when it was just getting light. I asked Captain Churchill where we were. 'I wish I knew,' he replied, 'we lost the swept channel two hours ago.' At 0600 I passed the news on to Monty who quickly got dressed and came up on deck. 'Lost, lost are we?' he ventured in the breeziest manner imaginable. He really was quite unperturbed.

Shortly afterwards a battleship, which luckily turned out to be American, was sighted. We soon found out from her that we had been swept down towards the Cherbourg peninsula. But, with the help of the signallers on board, it was not long before an escort arrived to take us up to the beaches. We could not have gone in on our own due to the possibility of encountering mines.

Soon we were off Omaha Beach and the height and steepness of the cliffs immediately struck us. General Omar Bradley was aboard USS *Augusta*. It was not difficult to find her as she was flying the American flag. Monty told me to go over to the *Augusta* to ask Bradley to come aboard the *Faulknor* for a talk.

I had no experience of jumping from a ship's steps into a small rocking boat on a rough sea. The dinghy seemed to be there one moment, and then it was not. But, somehow, I succeeded in climbing into the little boat without getting a soaking. A few minutes later I was being hauled

HMS Faulknor, *the destroyer that brought Monty across the Channel.* (IWM A6953)

up onto the *Augusta*'s deck for my meeting with the distinguished American general.

Bradley agreed to come to the *Faulknor* at once and reported to Monty that his troops had experienced a torrid time getting ashore and ascending the cliffs. Consequently the First American Army had so far made little progress.

After his talk with Bradley, Monty said that he wanted to see General Dempsey, the commander of the Second British Army. So we returned to the British sector, but could not find Dempsey's ship, HMS *Scylla*, immediately. Our superb signals contingent came to the rescue again and soon located her position. Dempsey then came aboard, bearing good news. His forward troops had got 7 or 8 miles inland. Almost at the same time, General Eisenhower and Admiral Ramsay arrived off the British sector in the latter's flagship and Monty was able to discuss the latest situation.

We then sailed back to the American sector to talk to Bradley again. Thankfully, his news was better. We returned to drop anchor off the British beaches and found the sea was a lot calmer. Before he retired to bed, Monty informed me that he wanted to land early in the morning. He told me to contact Noel Chavasse, who was now ashore, to arrange a 7 a.m. rendezvous.

Monty Sets Foot in France

Early in the morning on 8 June, at about 6.45, we set sail to move in close to the beaches to a given map reference point where Noel Chavasse would be waiting with an amphibious vehicle to bring Monty ashore. It was the first time I had ever seen Monty agitated. He was becoming increasingly impatient and kept telling me to get Captain Churchill to go in closer. Just as I was receiving an earful from the captain for interfering, there was a terrible shudder. The destroyer had clearly hit the bottom. Monty, who was by now both disappointed and frustrated, said, 'I suppose we can't go in any closer now.' But, luckily, Noel had seen us from the shore and promptly sent out a vehicle to collect us.

On landing, Monty was transferred to a jeep and driven to our Tac HQ, which had been set up in a field near Ste-Croix-sur-Mer. He went straight off to see Dempsey and it was then decided that the position of

Monty arrives in France on Juno Beach, 8 June. (Eton College Library)

our HQ was unsuitable. But, fortunately, Trumbull Warren, Monty's personal assistant, and one of our liaison officers, Carol Mather, had discovered a perfect spot on the edge of the garden of a lovely château at Creuilly, a small village a few miles east of Bayeux. The Tac HQ was transferred there the next afternoon, but not before Trum and Carol had found fifteen Germans hiding in a barn; they were taken prisoner at once.

Monty and a beachmaster in Normandy. (IWM B5175)

We stayed at Creuilly until 23 June and entertained some very distinguished guests there. Winston, Brooke, who was now a field marshal, and the South African Prime Minister, General Jan Smuts, visited on 12 June, and King George VI, who had come to Normandy to see the British and Canadian troops, arrived four days later.

A distinguished group at Creuilly. Left to right: Brooke, Churchill, Monty and Smuts. (Eton College Library)

Monty took more trouble with Brooke than any of his other visitors with the possible exception of the King. He was quite happy to leave the arrangements for anybody else, including Winston, to us, but always wanted to know all our plans for the CIGS. It was apparent that Monty very much knew that he owed his job to Brooke, whom he held in the highest regard.

Monty's Personal Staff in Europe

Several of the old guard had departed, so some new faces were needed at Monty's Tac HQ for the campaign in Europe. Indeed, in the end, we made up into quite a large contingent.

Monty's Tac HQ staff. Left to right: *Bon-Durant, Chavasse, Warren, Dawnay and the author.* (Eton College Library)

Kit Dawnay had joined us in February 1944 as Monty's military assistant. Monty had known Kit, who was a lieutenant-colonel in the Coldstream Guards, from his days with 3rd Division in 1940 and '41. He was much more a party to the fighting plans than we ADCs, and became a vital link between Monty and his commanders. He was the boss of Monty's personal staff, but was full of charm and had been lucky enough to marry Patsy Wake, whom I had always known. Kit immediately fitted in and contributed greatly to the happy atmosphere at our HQ.

Noel Chavasse, whose uncle of the same name was the only man to be awarded a double Victoria Cross in the First World War, was my fellow ADC and, like me, a captain. He had come back from Italy with Monty and had joined us at the end of our time in Sicily when John Poston was sent to the Staff College. Noel, whose father, the Bishop of Rochester, was an acquaintance of Monty, had been fighting with the Middlesex Regiment previously. He was in charge of Monty's cars and transport, while I was responsible for the mess and its staff. Otherwise we shared our general duties. Noel was full of energy and seldom relaxed. We got on fine, though life was never quite the same when John Poston left.

Trumbull Warren was a Canadian lieutenant-colonel who came as Monty's personal assistant. Trum was our contact with the Canadian Army. He got to know their commander, General Crerar, and his chief of staff extremely well and visited the Canadian contingent daily. Trum quickly became a close friend of all of us.

Ray Bon-Durant was an American captain personally chosen by Eisenhower to be an extra ADC to Monty. His particular role was to be a link between the American troops under Monty's command. Ray always travelled with Monty when he visited the Americans. He stayed with us after the breakout in Normandy, even though the American forces were then moved under the direction of General Bradley. Ray was a popular figure at our HQ.

About fifteen more staff were required to make the Tac HQ run smoothly. Corporal English, Monty's personal soldier servant, played a vital role. He looked after Monty splendidly, knowing all his whims and habits. Sergeant Ship was in charge of the mess and Sergeant Wright was the chef. When I was told to choose a chef from the Catering Corps, it seemed to me that we could get by on indifferent food if we had a good sauce. So I picked Johnny Wright, who had been a sauce chef at a well-known Soho restaurant before the war. He was tiny, about 5ft 4in, but was extremely jolly. We all went for a blow-out in his restaurant after the war and the food was quite delicious.

Then there were Sergeants Parker and Edwards, who drove the cars. Sergeant Parker always chauffeured the Rolls-Royce. Monty liked to sit all alone in the back so that he could do his thinking. I, on the other hand, travelled in the front, trying to find the right way with the map. There were also two typists. One of them, Sergeant Harwood, was very efficient and seemed to be given all the important jobs. Last but not least, each officer had an incredibly helpful soldier servant.

Sergeant Edwards (right) lovingly polishes Monty's Packard. (Eton College Library)

The pig that caused all the friction. (Eton College Library)

As our operation in Europe was so large, several other characters were attached to the Tac HQ in addition to Monty's personal staff. The team of liaison officers, which usually numbered between seven and eight, were based there. Also, there was an Operations set-up with Major Paul Odgers at its head. A first-class doctor, Bob Hunter, who became Lord Hunter after the war; Padre William Tindal, a charming Scottish Presbyterian minister; and a transport officer, George Butterworth, were around too. Finally, the camp commandant, Major Woodward, completed the cast list.

There was also a rather fastidious colonel who did not last long with Monty. Leo Russell, who, at the insistence of Freddie de Guingand, had been put in control of the LOs and in charge of an Ops room, sadly never fitted in. First, there were ructions among the LOs who had previously always reported directly to Monty. But, when Leo accused Monty of sanctioning the looting of a pig, which we later ate for dinner, from a French farmer, he had gone too far and was immediately sacked.

Freddie pleaded with Leo, but he still insisted on registering an official complaint against Monty. When Monty became CIGS in 1946, he discovered the relevant document in his personal file. He furiously ripped up the offending material and deposited the shreds of evidence in the waste-paper basket!

A Normal Day at Monty's European Tac HQ

Corporal English would call Monty at 6.30 every morning. Monty always said he did his thinking during the next hour. He would walk across to the mess tent at 8 – you could set your watch by it. Then he would go back to his day caravan where he usually had a talk with Kit Dawnay for twenty minutes. I would then come in and he would tell me the day's plans, suggest whom I should contact and arrange where and when we should meet. At about 9 a.m. he would see each of his liaison officers and give them instructions about which unit in the front line they should visit. By 10 Monty would want to know exactly what arrangements had been made. By 10.30 we were on our way.

In Normandy the distances were not very great, but, as we advanced through France, into Belgium, and then into Germany, the journeys became too far to go by road. So we had to travel by plane. Somehow the pilot always seemed to find an area nearby large enough to land on. We would always take a picnic lunch with enough sandwiches so that Monty could say to anyone present, 'Try one of these.'

We would usually be back between 3 and 4. He would then see Kit again and sometimes have a chat with Freddie de Guingand or Bill Williams. Miles Graham (Brian Robertson's successor as head of the Quartermaster's Department) or Jack Gannon, the military secretary who made all the appointments, would only come occasionally though. At around 5 p.m. the liaison officers would arrive back. Monty would spend the next hour or two with them, hearing first-hand news from the front line. The LOs would then mark up the position of every unit they had visited on a huge map. This was how Monty kept up to date with exactly what was happening in each sector.

Monty briefs his team of liaison officers. (Eton College Library)

Dinner, as always, was punctually at 8 p.m. and the next hour was kept for relaxation. Monty just wanted a lively discussion on a non-military subject that he would often choose. On one occasion Freddie and Bill flew over to Creuilly to see the chief and I remember thinking that their presence at dinner had well and truly livened up the party. Kit, Trum, Noel and I were therefore mildly surprised when, the next morning, Monty ordered us to talk more at dinner when we had guests! Quite

often we would have other visitors, although he did not like too many, but the conversation still never touched on army matters. At 9 on the dot Monty would leave for his night caravan, often commenting, 'The night is made for sleep.'

Of course, if something important happened, as it often did, we then had to depart from our normal routine.

The Liaison Officers

Monty rightly always wanted to know what was happening in the front line and did not want to be dependant on information from the relevant corps commanders. He had used his ADCs (John Poston and myself) in the desert to visit the divisional generals, brigade commanders and regimental colonels to obtain an up-to-date and accurate picture. But, as he had a much larger area to command in Europe, he decided to use a greater number of liaison officers, as they were known, to cover the whole front. Monty normally employed seven or eight personally picked officers of the rank of captain or major to perform this task. Their contribution was invaluable.

John Poston, who had rejoined Monty's entourage after attending the Staff College, was appointed a LO before the invasion of Europe. Carol Mather, who had been with Monty at Alamein and then joined David Stirling's SAS, was also employed in the same capacity. Carol had been captured in the desert and sent to a prisoner-of-war camp in northern Italy. When the Italians surrendered in September 1943, Carol managed to escape and somehow walked down through German-occupied territory. He eventually arrived at our HQ in the south after a six-week trek. Dick Harden, Charles Sweeny, who joined the group at the end of 1944, and Dudley Bouhill were three other British colleagues of John and Carol's, whom I got to know well. Two officers from the United States, Eddie Prisk and Maurice

The LOs. Left to right: Mather, Prisk, Sweeny, Frary, Bouhill, Harden and Poston (seated).
(Eton College Library)

Frary, who kept Monty in touch with the American front, completed the brave band.

De Gaulle

General de Gaulle returned to his homeland very shortly after D-Day. The first town he entered was Bayeux, where local crowds gathered round while he held out his arms as if he was their saviour. Traffic ground to a halt in the town centre as a result and the flow of army vehicles stopped.

When Monty heard, he said that de Gaulle must return to England and keep out of the way. When the request was made to de Gaulle, he said that France was his country and that he was not going to leave. So Monty sent a message to Churchill through Freddie de Guingand asking for the General to be removed. The answer came back that de Gaulle must be allowed to stay.

I remember thinking at the time that de Gaulle was the only Frenchman I had ever been able to understand. He spoke his native tongue so slowly and deliberately that even I, with my dreadful French, could make an adequate translation of virtually everything he said.

The Miles Messenger

One day Monty received a letter from the Miles aircraft company, offering a small plane for his use in France. He liked the idea and I was told to make arrangements for its delivery. Of course, it was necessary to employ a pilot. So Flying Officer Trevor Martin joined our HQ to take up the post. Monty used the Miles Messenger extensively and it was also very useful for transporting visitors back and forth.

Fortunately, I was not with Monty when he experienced a nasty scare in

Monty and de Gaulle. (Eton College Library)

the Miles Messenger on a visit to the 3rd Canadian Division in Germany in August 1945 after the war. As the plane was circling the airfield, the engine cut out and the pilot was forced to crash-land in a field nearby. The aircraft was completely written off, but the pilot and another passenger somehow emerged completely unhurt. Monty, however, was not so lucky. He was severely shaken and badly bruised and was eventually found to have broken two lumbar vertebrae.

Monty bravely began to address the Canadian officers but had to stop half-way through the speech, as he felt so ill. His hosts offered to provide a car to take him back to his HQ, but he insisted on flying in another little aircraft. The Canadians did not like the idea, but Monty told them not to worry, arguing that nobody had ever been involved in a plane crash twice in the same day!

Monty and his pilot, Trevor Martin, pose beside the Miles Messenger aircraft.
(Eton College Library)

Monty photographed at a press conference in Normandy. (IWM B5536)

The Media Reveal Too Much

Great preparations had been made at Creuilly for the visit of the King at noon on 16 June. He was a little short and sharp on his arrival, having had a rough journey, but soon warmed up. Sadly, he was not allowed to travel elsewhere, as there were still snipers about.

After the King arrived back in England that night, it was announced on the radio that he had been to see Monty at his HQ in the grounds of a château. A similar article in the *Daily Mail* also did its best to tell the enemy where we were based. Our fears that the press had injudiciously pointed out our exact position to the Germans were realised when we were heavily shelled less than a week later. For safety reasons, our Tac HQ was then moved immediately to Blaye, 6 miles west of Bayeux.

Dempsey, the King and Monty at Creuilly. (Eton College Library)

The Politician who Dared to Speak his Mind

After we had heard the good news that the Americans had cut off the top half of the Cherbourg peninsula, I went to pick up Sir James Grigg at one of the landing strips at noon on 18 June. The Secretary of State for War lunched at Creuilly and then went with Monty to the 11th Armoured Division and VIII Corps HQs during the afternoon. He flew back to England at 1930 hours, laden with some delicious and strong-smelling Camembert cheeses.

I remember thinking how genuine Sir James was and how much he wanted to help. He was very much to the point and was not afraid to

The Secretary of State for War, Sir James Grigg, and Monty. (Eton College Library)

say what he thought of his political colleagues and opponents. That was probably why he was relatively unpopular in a world that is not renowned for plain speaking. He was also most interested to find out why the French people were showing so little enthusiasm for the Allied invasion and laid much of the blame at de Gaulle's feet. Indeed, he was adamant that the General was not the man to give France a lead.

How wrong the Secretary of State turned out to be!

A Narrow Escape

Two days later, I travelled with Monty to XXX Corps HQ. While he was choosing new commanding officers for the five regiments, which had recently lost their colonels, with the XXX Corps chief, General Bucknall, three Bf109s (Messerschmitt fighter aircraft) came over a hedge

A Messerschmitt Bf109. (IWM MH6116)

at zero feet and sprayed the camp with machine-gun fire. Fortunately, they missed the caravan Monty was in by inches.

A Religious Problem

25 June was a boiling day that turned out to be extremely eventful. I flew with Monty in the Miles Messenger to VIII Corps to discuss forthcoming plans with General O'Connor in the early morning. When we landed next to their HQ in a small field, surrounded by high mature hedges, I wondered how we would ever get out again. I had good cause to be worried, as we only just managed to clear the trees when we took off on the return flight.

Later that morning, we had a delightful service conducted by Padre Hughes in the tiny church in Blaye village. Our Chaplain-General had previously expressed anxiety that a scandal might arise because we had used a Roman Catholic place of worship for a Protestant service. Monty, however, said that he was all for it and was ready for any showdown that might entail. It transpired that the padre was absolutely right to be concerned. When the Roman Catholic chaplains eventually found out about our service a week later, they complained vociferously and even asked the Bishop of Bayeux to put a stop to any more. I am ashamed to say we all looked forward to the start of a first-class ecclesiastical row!

Padre Hughes, who concluded the controversial Blaye service, with Monty. (Eton College Library)

After dinner, I went out with John Poston and Dick Harden on a night patrol in search of chickens. We captured six plump hens after a grand hunt in a coop belonging to a local farmer, who luckily remained asleep during the rather noisy proceedings.

I dropped off very quickly that night and dreamt sweetly of our successful chase in the moonlight.

'Hitler' and 'Rommel'

We were having dinner in the mess at our Tac HQ at Blaye in late June, when Monty suddenly said that he would like a dog. He suggested that it might be worth asking Frank Gillard, the BBC's distinguished war

Monty at play with 'Hitler' (left) and 'Rommel'. (Eton College Library)

correspondent, to announce on the wireless that he was looking for one. Frank, who became head of BBC Radio after the war, agreed to help immediately, but our public relations department, probably quite correctly, put a stop to the broadcast on the grounds that it was too trivial a topic for wartime.

I began to rack my brains for another way to obtain a canine friend for Monty, but I need not have worried. My prayers were more than answered when, a few days later on 1 July, Kit Dawnay came back from England, cradling the tiniest golden King Charles spaniel puppy for the chief. Later that evening, I could hardly believe my luck when Frank Gillard also arrived with a perfect little Jack Russell terrier pup as a gift from all the BBC representatives in Normandy.

The Prime Minister makes friends with 'Rommel'. (Eton College Library)

Monty, rather bizarrely we all thought, insisted on naming the spaniel 'Rommel' and the terrier 'Hitler'. But he adored the new younger members of our Tac HQ and played with the two small dogs whenever he had a free moment.

An Impromptu Afternoon Nap

On 2 July I went with Monty to the Guards Armoured Division base where he gave a talk on the state of the campaign in Normandy to high ranking officers. We were having a cup of tea after returning to Blaye, when he looked me straight in the eye and said, 'You couldn't have

German prisoners gape at Monty as his Jeep passes by. (Eton College Library)

thought what I was saying much good, I saw that you were fast asleep.'
Feeling extremely awkward, I quickly left the table, pretending I had
an urgent chore to attend to.

The Snake in the Grass

A row between the Air Force and the Army, which had been simmering
for some time, finally came to a head in early July. Coningham, the head
of Tactical Air Forces, was the snake in the grass, playing dirty games
behind the Army's back and refusing to cooperate with Monty. The
problem was that Coningham viewed capturing the airfields south-east
of Caen as the main priority rather than helping Monty and the Army
defeat Rommel. The chief, however, rightly felt that, when the Battle

of Normandy was won, everything else would follow, including those airfields. Furthermore, it did not help that Leigh-Mallory, the air commander, and Coningham did not get on.

Therefore, when Arthur Tedder (the British Air Chief Marshal who was Ike's deputy) visited the Tac HQ at Blaye, Monty took the bull by the horns and told him that the Army was not getting the best support from the air due to Coningham's unhelpful attitude. He also added that this problem was affecting the progress of the whole campaign. Heaven knows what Tedder said to 'Mary' Coningham, but the latter was over here the next day, almost in tears, and only too anxious to help.

I recall wondering, rather cynically, how long this new blissful state of affairs would last. Unfortunately, the answer was a very short period indeed. An entry in my diary for 19 July, the day before our troops finally cleared Caen's eastern suburbs, reveals that Monty told the CIGS, Brooke, that the Army had no confidence in Coningham and that it was absolutely vital that Leigh-Mallory remained as air commander-in-chief.

Left to right: *Dempsey, Crerar, Monty, Simpson and Coningham – the snake in the grass.* (IWM B14020)

The author and Monty surrounded by French citizens at Caen Cathedral. (Eton College Library)

A Plan to Dispose of Rommel

On 16 July 'Boy' Browning approached Monty with a bizarre, but interesting, scheme. We were all surprised when the colourful head of all the airborne divisions asked the chief if he would like to have Rommel bumped off. Browning went on to explain that he had found the German commander's HQ by dropping the odd parachutist behind enemy lines and that he now knew where Rommel went to pursue two of his favourite hobbies, fishing and shooting pigeons. Well aware of his great rival's considerable military talents and believing that Rommel's demise would make his own task in Normandy much easier, Monty answered in the affirmative. So General Browning promised that he would make the necessary arrangements.

Of course, history relates that this ambitious plan never succeeded.

'Boy' Browning, the dashing airborne forces commander. (IWM H. 24128)

Casualties

Although they were sadly inevitable in war, Monty was always extremely concerned about casualties. Indeed, one of his military assistant Kit Dawnay's most important jobs in Europe was to keep him completely up to date with the figures. Monty not only wanted to know the number killed and wounded, but also which divisions the men were in, and which regiments they belonged to. He also insisted on regular reports on Allied and enemy tank losses.

The figures below, which Kit produced during the Battle of Normandy, give some idea of the terrible damage the campaign inflicted on the Allied forces and prove that Monty's dictum, 'Fighting is not cheap', was absolutely true.

10 July	British	Killed 3,894	Wounded 18,314
	American	Killed 6,898	Wounded 32,443

German prisoners are marched to a Mulberry harbour off the Normandy coast. (Eton College Library)

Yet, only nine days later, the total casualty figures for the Normandy campaign had risen substantially.

| 19 July | British | Killed 6,010 | Wounded 28,690 |
| | American | Killed 10,641 | Wounded 51,387 |

The number of Allied casualties, however, had nearly doubled when another count was taken twenty-three days later as the Battle of Normandy was drawing to a close.

| 11 August | British and Canadian | 68,000 |
| | American | 102,000 |

Of course, Monty was also well aware that very heavy losses and lack of reinforcements were a crucial factor in the speed of the Allied advance. He knew better than anyone that there were no more fighting men left at home in Britain, the United States and Canada.

Winston and Brooke Come to the Forest of Cerisy

When Churchill and Brooke visited our Tac HQ in the Forest of Cerisy in early August 1944, rumours were spreading that Monty was going to be removed and replaced by Alex as head of 21st Army Group. As soon as the Prime Minister and the CIGS arrived, Monty took them into his map caravan and revealed his plans. His aim had always been to draw the German armour onto the British flank in the east, thus allowing the American to break out in the west.

It was well known that Eisenhower did not properly understand Monty's plan and that Tedder had been pouring poison into the Supreme Commander's ear about the inability of the British to move forward. But, although the British Army was behind the schedule set for the first two months of the Normandy campaign, Monty explained that his strategy was working and assured Winston and Brooke that victory was not far away. In the end they accepted Monty's argument. Consequently dinner that evening was a jovial affair.

Monty and Brooke. (IWM B5366)

Ike, Monty and Tedder. (IWM B5562)

James Gunn

Augustus John's failure to capture his likeness on canvas did not deter Monty, and, after much consultation, he was now persuaded that James Gunn was the best portrait painter of the time. So the famous artist was invited out to our HQ in the Forest of Cerisy to paint Monty in mid-August. He had only been with us a few days and had not done enough sittings to finish the portrait when an Allied breakthrough on the front around Falaise seemed imminent. When that decisive day in the Battle of Normandy finally arrived and the advance of the British,

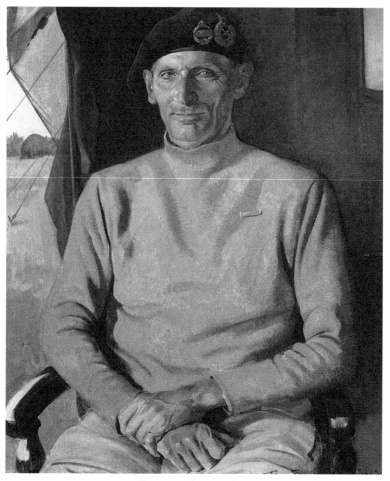

Sir James Gunn's portrait of Monty. (IWM HU44413)

Gunn's picture of Monty and his staff in the mess. Clockwise: *Monty, Dawnay, Bon-Durant, the author, Warren and Chavasse.* (Eton College Library)

American and Canadian forces commenced, Monty's Tac HQ had to move to Campeaux, near Le Bény-Bocage. So James came along with us.

One afternoon soon after, Monty rang the bell for me. But I did not hear it immediately. In fact, I was sitting for James, who had kindly agreed to paint my portrait as a thank-you for looking after him during the move. When I eventually answered Monty's call, he said, 'Johnny, where on earth were you?' 'In the mess tent with James,' I replied, 'as he has said he would like to paint me.' Monty retorted angrily, 'Send him to me immediately. He is here to paint me, not you.'

So that was the end of my portrait. James, however, did manage to complete a drawing of me when Monty had gone out one day. He also painted a wonderful picture of Monty and his personal staff in the mess, which was bought later by King George VI. It hung for many years at the bottom of the stairs during the Queen Mother's time at Clarence House and is still in the same place now that the Prince of Wales has taken up residence there.

The Church at Aunay-sur-Odon

Shortly after the Allied breakthrough in Normandy, I flew with Monty over the area south of Caen known as the Falaise Pocket, where the heaviest fighting and air raids had taken place. There was carnage

The church at Aunay-sur-Odon. (Eton College Library)

Devastation in the Norman town of Condé. (Eton College Library)

everywhere. Thousands of enemy prisoners were on the move and many of their dead and wounded were still lying where they had fallen. There were burnt-out or abandoned tanks and vehicles on every road and dead horses decaying in the boiling sun. It was a harrowing and desolate scene and the smell of death hung heavily in the sultry summer air.

Our plane also passed over Aunay-sur-Odon in the Calvados département of Lower Normandy, which had been heavily bombed a week after D-Day. The small town had suffered the most terrible damage. All the houses and shops were razed to the ground, but the tall steeple of the church had somehow survived the endless bombardment. The extraordinary sight of this symbol of God, still standing in splendid isolation among the ruins, simply took our breath away.

SIX

THRUST INTO
GERMANY

20 AUGUST 1944–4 MAY 1945

The shattered German forces in France were in a desperate state and the speed of the Allied advance after the Battle of Normandy was staggering. The Americans reached Paris on 24 August and the British liberated Brussels on 4 September. Monty wanted to keep the momentum going and believed that a concentrated thrust through Belgium and Holland to Germany's industrial heartlands of the Ruhr was the quickest way to end the war in Europe. Eisenhower, however, favoured splitting his forces and moving forward on a much broader front towards Germany. Therefore he ordered 21st Army Group to head north through Belgium and Holland and 12th Army Group to go west via Metz towards the River Saar. Monty continued to argue long and hard for his plan, but Ike refused to change his mind.

The Allies' progress was not so smooth during the late autumn of 1944 and the following winter. The Germans regrouped and launched a spirited defence of the Fatherland. The unexpected resistance from a refitting Panzer group, which drove the British back from the vital Arnhem bridgehead in late September, and von Rundstedt's heavy offensive that pierced a huge salient or bulge in the fragile American line at the Battle of the Ardennes in December, certainly surprised the Allied commanders and prolonged the war.

After Monty, who had taken over the command of all American forces north of the bulge, organised a successful counter-attack, the lengthy Battle of the Ardennes was over by 16 January 1945. By the end of March, the Allies, having crossed the Rhine in strength, were fighting deep in Germany and, as the Russians were moving in fast from the east, the enemy was under pressure from all sides. It was now only a matter of time before the war in Europe ended. Monty was disappointed not to reach Berlin before the Red Army, but was delighted to sign the Instrument of Surrender of all German armed forces on 4 May at Lüneburg Heath.

Monty crosses a bridge on the advance through north-west Europe. (IWM BU551)

The Promotion to Field Marshal

It was 1 September at our Tac HQ at the Château de Dangu, north of the Seine, when Kit Dawnay told me that Monty had heard that he been promoted to the rank of field marshal.

When I saw Monty later that morning, I said, 'I have just heard the news. I am so glad. Many congratulations.' There was no reply – it was as if he had not heard me. Perhaps he was too embarrassed to answer or too preoccupied. I don't know, but it was not in his nature to say nothing. That evening, however, Monty was on great form at dinner. I had suggested to Kit that we should produce a bottle of wine to drink the new field marshal's health, but he, probably rightly, thought Monty would not like the idea.

Monty received his field marshal's baton from the King at Buckingham Palace on 7 November on his next visit to England.

A harsh penalty. (Eton College Library)

The Penalty for Collaboration

The French sheared off the hair of any unfortunate girl caught cohabiting with a German soldier. This harsh form of rough justice, which was always exacted in front of jeering crowds, was a regular sight as we passed through towns and cities during the liberation of France.

The Liberation of Brussels

The British Army received an unbelievable reception when it entered Brussels on 4 September. Girls climbed on vehicles, everybody cheered and the champagne flowed. It was a quite remarkable sight. Just before the British went into the city, they sought out a small Belgian contingent so that they could enter together. That was a nice touch and much

Joyful celebrations as the British enter Brussels. (Eton College Library)

appreciated by the locals. When Monty arrived shortly afterwards, we were told to go to the Hôtel de Ville (the town hall) where the burgomaster (the chief magistrate) would greet us. Again there was lots of shouting and Monty got a fabulous reception. It was a really happy occasion.

One young Belgian officer, who had been smothered in kisses, later went to visit his mother, who lived in Brussels. When she came out to greet her long-lost son, she flung her arms around him and asked, 'Oh my poor darling, where have you been wounded?' He quickly dispelled her worries, explaining that it was not blood all over his face but the local girls' lipstick!

The Relationship with Eisenhower

From the first time he met Eisenhower in the desert after the capture of Tripoli, Monty very much liked and admired the American general. Monty first served under Ike during the Sicily campaign, when the latter was overall commander of the British and American forces. They combined well during the planning for the invasion of Sicily and for the five weeks of fighting, which culminated in the occupation of the island. Their good relationship continued during the invasion of Italy and the Allied advance northwards up the mainland. During this time Ike let Monty get on with the job and never interfered. The atmosphere whenever they met was most congenial and they became good friends.

When Monty returned to England to command the Normandy landings, he was

Ike and Monty in a brief moment of relaxation together.
(Eton College Library)

delighted to find that Ike had been appointed as the Supreme Commander and was happy with his own position as commander of the British, American and Canadian forces during the invasion of France. Monty also agreed with the decision that the Allied command should be split after the breakthrough in Normandy had been achieved and when progress in France was forward enough. He was content to remain in charge of the British and Canadian forces and to let Bradley take over the United States armies.

Left to right: *the author, Ike, Monty and Butcher take tea and biscuits.*
(Eton College Library)

After about two months of fighting in Normandy, little progress was being made. Consequently, Winston began to get impatient. Tedder, Ike's deputy, was in the same state of mind as the Prime Minister. So the two began to prod Eisenhower to take some action and there was even talk of Monty being replaced by Alexander. This was the first time Ike had questioned Monty's plan, which was to push with the British forces on the eastern flank, thus drawing the German reserves into that area, and then break through with the American forces in the west. Monty was annoyed that Ike appeared to distrust his tactical judgement and began to say that he was a political rather than a fighting general. That, of course, was what Eisenhower really was.

Shortly afterwards, when the breakthrough occurred and a large number of German troops surrendered in the Falaise Pocket, good relations between Monty and Ike were restored. The German Army was now in retreat. The advance was swift with the British soon entering Brussels and the Americans Paris. The split in command between Monty and Bradley now took place.

The result of the fast Allied advance was that the supply lines soon became stretched. Monty then came to the conclusion that the only way to end the war quickly was with one solid push in the northern sector, which was under his command, towards Germany's industrial belt around the River Ruhr. As American forces and their transport would be needed to supply such an operation, their advance in the south would have to be halted. Monty pressed Ike with this plan again and again and became increasingly frustrated that Eisenhower, rather than he, was in charge of the campaign and therefore had the last word.

One could understand Ike supporting the idea if it was the only course of action, but it would have been neither politic nor diplomatic for the Supreme Commander to halt the American advance further south to support Monty's planned foray into Germany. Ike became irritated that Monty would not accept that the thrust towards the Ruhr was just not on, but his calm and generous attitude towards an increasingly persistent Monty certainly stopped any major difficulties arising at the time. I should also add that Freddie de Guingand's close friendship with Ike and his Chief of Staff, Bedell Smith, helped to calm these potentially troubled waters.

Some Other Possible Explanations for Arnhem

Monty, who was in charge of the operation, Ike, who, as Supreme Commander, gave the go-ahead for the daring raid, and many military historians have all described the famous failure to hold the bridge over the Neder Rijn at Arnhem. They have also examined the tragic reasons why only 2,400 out of the 9,000 men of the British 1st Airborne Division returned, when Monty was forced to order their withdrawal on 25 September after an unexpected and powerful counter-attack by II SS Panzer Corps, which was then refitting in that part of Holland. Therefore, this major Allied catastrophe, which ended in such terrible loss of life, has probably had more than its fair share of coverage, but the following observations might still be worth making.

I recall that Monty was put under considerable pressure by 'Boy' Browning, the airborne forces' commander, to go ahead with the assault on Arnhem. Browning continuously pointed out that the British division needed to see some action quickly because their morale was extremely low, thanks to many of their planned operations being scrapped due to the speed of the Allied advance after the Battle of Normandy. 'Boy' Browning's arguments swayed Monty and certainly contributed to the latter's decision to send the 1st Airborne into Arnhem when he did, even though the weather forecast was bad and his intelligence sources had identified that a substantial German force was in the vicinity.

The famous bridge at Arnhem, photographed from an RAF reconnaissance aircraft. (IWM MH2061)

The loss of the bridgehead is often said to have prolonged the war by six months, as the Allies consequently failed to gain possession of the vital area between Arnhem and the Zuider Zee from where the next leg of the advance into north Germany would have been launched. But it should also be pointed out that the rest of Operation Market Garden, of which the Arnhem initiative was only a part, was a success and liberated a large part of Holland. The two American airborne divisions, allocated to Monty by Eisenhower for the project, fulfilled their objectives, taking two vital bridges over the Meuse at Grave and the Waal at Nijmegen. But, as all the publicity at the time inevitably centred on the disaster at Arnhem, Monty's reputation as a battle commander, which had been sky high after Normandy, certainly deteriorated, and his strategy was even criticised later by his great advocate, Field Marshal Brooke.

Monty's pride was obviously dented, but it must have hurt much more when he eventually discovered that he was a little unlucky that the

Arnhem part of his grand design to grab this important bit of Holland did not work. Of course, if the 1st Airborne had landed nearer the bridge and the weather had then relented to allow much-needed reinforcements to be parachuted in, our troops might still have been able to repel the enemy, despite the presence of the Panzers.

But it is also possible that there would have been a totally different scenario if Eisenhower had not hesitated over Monty's plan to keep up the momentum of the Allied advance and called a brief halt that autumn. When our forces retook Arnhem much later, Carol Mather was told by a local resident that it was a great pity that the first Allied assault had not been launched two weeks earlier, as there were then no German forces in the locality. Apparently, the enemy, terrified by the speed with which we were moving, had fled, and only returned when the coast appeared to be clear.

Hindsight always makes events easier to analyse, but it appears that the main reason for the reversal at Arnhem was simply timing. If Ike had not been so indecisive and we had got there a fortnight before, it is likely that we would have been celebrating a great victory rather than mourning a costly defeat.

The King Comes to Stay at Eindhoven

As we had been feeling very low since Arnhem, there was great excitement at our Tac HQ at Eindhoven later that autumn when we were told that King George VI was coming to see us. The weather in Holland was so bad that his trip had to be postponed for a day or two, but eventually conditions improved enough to allow his plane to land at 1300 hours on 11 October.

The King visited the Second British Army the next day, the Canadians the day after, and the First US Army on the 14th, when he lunched with Eisenhower. The King certainly had a busy schedule, but he was delighted to be able to mingle with the troops. He also told us that he relished sleeping in a caravan for a few days and that he had not felt so unrestricted or relaxed since the beginning of the war.

The first night the King arrived, one of his equerries walked over to Freddie de Guingand's caravan and asked quietly if he had a bottle of

The author receives his MBE from the King at the end of the war. (Eton College Library)

whisky. Apparently the King was longing for a drink, but, knowing Monty was teetotal, was worried that no alcohol would be served in the mess at dinner. Freddie was delighted to hand over a bottle of the hard stuff and sent a message back to assure the King that there would be plenty of wine at the table, too.

Monty had asked the King if he would present a number of decorations during his visit. As enemy gunfire could be heard in the background, it was a strange feeling, as well as a great honour, to receive my MBE from the sovereign at our Tac HQ on the morning of 15 October. Also, Freddie and Miles Dempsey were knighted in what turned out to be a ceremony of some historical significance. Freddie was delighted to be informed that no reigning monarch had bestowed such an accolade on a soldier in the field of battle since Henry V at Agincourt in 1415.

The King was due to fly back to England at 2 p.m., but the weather turned foul again and his departure had to be delayed. As nothing was planned for the afternoon, I asked the King if he would like to join

Monty briefs the King at Tac HQ at Eindhoven. (Eton College Library)

me for a game of golf at the local course at Eindhoven. He accepted with alacrity, so I invited the professional golfer, Dai Rees, to make up a threesome.

As Dai was then employed as the driver for the commander of the supporting air force group, whose headquarters were conveniently in the clubhouse, he knew the little course like the back of his hand. The King and I obviously could not match Dai's incredible skill, but we enjoyed playing a few holes with the famous Welsh sportsman, who was later to become the most proficient match player in Britain. Indeed, the King told me afterwards that Dai had passed on some useful tips to improve the royal swing.

An unforgettable day ended with a farewell dinner that included a first course of oysters. We had to be up early to bid this charming but shy monarch a fond farewell. But, as the weather refused to relent, the King was forced to abandon his aeroplane and return to England by sea from Ostend in a naval destroyer.

The Doodlebug

From late October to mid-November, after we had moved from Holland back to Belgium, Monty was lent a substantial house in Brussels by the local authorities. Whenever we were in residence there, a soldier was always positioned on the roof to warn us if a doodlebug (a self-propelling airborne bomb that exploded when the engine cut out) was approaching. The lookout's job was to press a button which rang a bell in Monty's office. One day a doodlebug came a little too close for comfort and the poor soldier ducked and forgot to press his button. A huge explosion in the garden at the back of the house followed, and all the windows shattered.

I was in our office at the time. So I rushed upstairs to see if Monty was all right. I found him calmly sitting at his desk draped in a net curtain.

Monty's mansion in Brussels. (Eton College Library)

A V1 flying bomb, otherwise known as a doodlebug, heads on its dangerous path earthwards.
(IMW HU636)

Thank goodness that the curtain had been hanging over the window. It prevented the broken glass from entering the room and stopped Monty from being injured. He was quite unperturbed by this near miss and carried on as if nothing had happened.

Hot Coffee – A Successful Bet

One day in the very cold winter of 1944–5, Monty happened to visit a battalion of the 60th Rifles under the command of Robin Hastings,

Dick Harden (left), Monty and the author stop for a coffee break. (Eton College Library)

Toby Wake (far right) sits next to the author at dinner. (Eton College Library)

whom I knew. Robin suggested that I go over and have dinner one evening as they were out of the line for a short period. I accepted his invitation and found many friends, among them Toby Wake.

During dinner Toby got up to go out to relieve himself. Robin said that it amazed him how often Toby, who never touched alcohol and, for that matter, still does not, went on this errand. I answered, 'Well, my man, Monty, has exactly the same habit.'

Then we struck a bet. On a chosen day, a week hence, the man whose nominee peed more times between 8 a.m. and 6 p.m. would be the winner. We could do anything to improve our candidate's score but, of course, it was forbidden to tell Monty or Toby about the wager.

Later I told Corporal English about the bet. He agreed to keep a close eye on Monty and help make the count. Then, before we set off for wherever we were going that day, I had some hot coffee put in the

car. It was extremely cold, but my principal purpose was to make Monty drink plenty of liquid. Before we reached our destination, I asked Monty if he would like to stop for a cup. This we did and my plan seemed to work. For, when we finished our journey, the first thing Monty asked was, 'Where is the lavatory?'

By the end of the day Monty's score was six pees. So I sent Robin a signal, declaring my tally. He soon replied that his candidate had only managed five. Some months later I bumped into Robin, who promptly paid up his debt.

Monty liked the idea of the hot coffee and consequently a thermos was placed in the car every day in the winter. But, when I owned up that the whole idea had started as a result of a bet, he did not seem greatly amused.

A Masterly Performance

Alamein is generally rated as Monty's greatest victory, but his performance in the Ardennes in southern Belgium in the winter of 1944–45 should also number among his finest military achievements.

Monty lunches with US Generals Simpson (left) and Collins.
(Eton College Library)

Field Marshal von Rundstedt (nearest the camera), the German commander who caused such problems in the Ardennes. (IWM EA7205)

Two Allied thrusts were being made that December by Bradley's 12th US Army Group towards Cologne and the Saar river respectively at either end of its 150-mile front. As the front was so long, its middle in the Ardennes was sparsely defended and represented its weakest point. So there was always a danger that a German counter-attack would breach this fragile area in the line, especially as Bradley was finding it hard to control both wings from his HQ in Luxembourg. Sure enough, the German commander, von Rundstedt, realised that Bradley's army was overstretched and launched a powerful offensive through the Ardennes towards the River Meuse on 16 December.

The attack caught the Americans by surprise and a strong wedge, or salient, was driven through the middle of the Twelfth Army front, isolating the Ninth and First US Armies in the north and the Third US Army and Bradley's HQ in the south. The Americans tried to plug the gaps, but the front was far too wide and it was obvious by 18 December that the Germans had achieved a major breakthrough.

As soon as Monty, whose forces were positioned on the immediate left of the Ninth Army, saw what was happening, he took precautions to stop the Germans crossing the Meuse and sent XXX Corps into the locality between Louvain and Gembloux to safeguard the British area. He also stationed reconnaissance patrols on bridges over the Meuse that lay outside his own sector. As he had kept in close touch with the battle north of the bulge through his liaison officers, Monty knew that the morale of the First and Ninth US Armies was low and that its commanding officers were unsure what action to take, as neither Bradley nor any of his HQ staff had issued any orders or had been near this part of the front.

Consequently Monty was acutely aware that matters were deteriorating when Eisenhower telephoned at 10.30 hours on 20 December and put the First and Ninth US Armies under his command. Monty moved fast and within an hour we were on our way to see General Hodges of the First US Army and General Simpson of the Ninth US Army. Contrary to some reports that I later read, Hodges and Simpson were actually extremely pleased to see their new commander and visibly relieved to be given clear and concise instructions.

Monty quickly made some important changes to relieve the pressure on the Americans. He put British soldiers under the command of the Ninth Army to fight alongside the Americans and made the Ninth Army take over those bits of the First Army front where the fighting had been particularly ferocious. He also brought in British forces as reserves behind the two American armies, until they were able to create their own. Monty's sound new strategy meant that the situation was slowly and carefully restored and the Germans were eventually driven back by 16 January.

Monty's tactics in the Ardennes were virtually faultless, but I have always believed that the strong leadership and encouragement he gave to the downcast Americans, from commanding officers down to troops, and the confidence he instilled in them on his regular visits to the front were the major reasons why the tide turned.

Rubbing Salt in Bradley's Wounds

At the end of 1944 Monty was confident of success in the Ardennes and was inclined to crow privately that he had pulled Bradley and the Americans out of a deep hole. I think it is also fair to say that he felt that recent events had confirmed his long-held opinion that a single head of land forces was required in the Allied command set-up and that he was the man for the job. Anyhow, the British press began to push this line and lionised Monty as the man who had saved the day after an American general had failed to deliver. Naturally, the American journalists sprang to Bradley's defence and portrayed him as the hero of the conflict, which they prefer to call the Battle of the Bulge. Bradley's troops, however, received plenty of British newspapers, so there was a real danger that his men might lose confidence in their leader.

Freddie de Guingand, after obtaining a report from a liaison officer on the strength of feeling in Bradley's HQ over the articles in the British papers, realised that it was time to intervene. So he flew to France to the SHAEF headquarters at Versailles to try to smooth things over with Eisenhower.

It was lucky for Monty that Freddie decided to act because he found the Supreme Commander in a state of shock. Ike pointed out that Bradley's position was intolerable and enquired whether Monty realised how damaging the British press's campaign had become. He added that Monty had created the crisis by his repeated indiscreet remarks that a single land commander was needed. Ike then dropped a bombshell. He showed Freddie a signal that he had prepared, informing the Combined Chiefs of Staff that he had decided that it was impossible for himself and Monty to continue working together.

Freddie realised that Monty would be fired if this message was sent, as America was the more powerful ally. So he pleaded with Ike to give him a chance to put things right. When Freddie returned to our HQ near Zonhoven on 31 December, Monty was amazed and extremely worried to hear that he was in such a precarious position. But he immediately agreed to send an apologetic signal to Ike, which fortunately had the desired effect.

Monty had escaped the sack by the skin of his teeth, but he did not learn his lesson. In a press conference on 7 January 1945 he exacerbated

Bradley (right), Monty and Dempsey in less confrontational times. (IWM B5320)

the row with Bradley using the occasion as an opportunity to pat himself on the back, and, worse, adopting a patronising tone. This did not help Bradley and undermined his position even more. Monty even referred to the Ardennes battle as 'interesting', which understandably drove the Americans mad as they had borne the brunt of the heavy casualties

Bradley never forgave Monty. Indeed, for the rest of his life he continued to perpetuate the myth that the Battle of the Bulge was an American triumph. In a sense, Bradley had the last laugh. Historians and commentators in the United States have never given Monty any credit for the victory in the Ardennes and have used the American general's version of events ever since.

Winston Crossing the Rhine

As soon as it was decided that 21st Army Group would cross the Rhine in strength on 23 March, a message arrived from Winston saying that he would like to be there. When he arrived at our Tac HQ at a riding school at Straelen in Germany, we were told that the Prime Minister would also like to cross to the eastern side of the river.

He was duly taken to the west bank of the Rhine near the town of Wesel on 25 March, but it was decided that it was too dangerous to go over as there was still long-distance shelling in the area. Suddenly we noticed Winston, who had escaped from all around him, climbing up the side of the bombed-out railway bridge. This gallant attempt to traverse

A determined Churchill escapes from his minders across the rubble of a destroyed German bridge.
(Eton College Library)

Churchill and Monty cross to the Rhine's east bank in an American amphibious vehicle.
(US National Archives)

the river was quickly thwarted by his nervous aides on safety grounds. But eventually he was able to travel across in a landing craft.

I remember the Prime Minister was in excellent spirits that night at dinner and delighted to have set foot on German soil on the east bank of the Rhine. During the meal, in order to provoke an argument, Monty asked his guests and members of his staff for their definition of a gentleman. When Winston was asked, he replied, 'I know one when I see one,' and then quickly added, 'Someone who is only rude intentionally.' Monty thought that was a masterly answer and often repeated the Prime Minister's definition in the future.

There was also a good story going around at the time that Winston had fulfilled a long-held ambition to pee into the Rhine. That may be true, but I am unable to confirm or deny that the Prime Minister satisfied his wish!

John Poston's Death

On 21 April, not long before the end of the war, John Poston was returning by jeep from the front with another liaison officer, Peter Earle. They were not far from our HQ when suddenly a group of Germans jumped out of a ditch and opened fire. John, his Sten gun empty, was killed by an enemy soldier's bayonet during the skirmish. But Peter, although wounded by bullets in the arm and temple, somehow managed to survive and relayed the bad news the next day.

That was the only time I saw Monty very distressed. He was extremely fond of John, who had been with him since he started with the Eighth Army. John's funeral took place in the field at Soltau in Lower Saxony where our caravans were parked. It was a sad and most moving ceremony and, like all of us, Monty unashamedly wept.

John Poston's grave at Soltau. (Eton College Library)

Padre Tindal, who conducted John Poston's funeral service. (Eton College Library)

Padre Tindal's short but poignant address summed up exactly how we all felt about losing John, who was only 25 years old:
'We commit his body to rest in the earth, but we know that for his restless, eager spirit, there is life and activity in the world beyond.

We bid him farewell, but in dying he shares his life with us, and we know ourselves richer because he lived.

We think of our cause, and glimpse again its greatness as we look at John Poston and the great company of his brethren who have yielded their lives for us.'

The Surrender

The telephone rang in our little tent on the side of Monty's day caravan on Lüneburg Heath, about 30 miles south-east of Hamburg, on the morning of 3 May. It was Corps HQ who said they had a party of four German officers there, who claimed that they had come to surrender all their armed forces on behalf of Admiral Dönitz, who was now the overall commander. Corps HQ added that they believed the delegation was *bona fide* as one member was an admiral, who really looked the part in his smart naval uniform.

'Hold on,' I replied, 'while I go and inform Monty.' Monty told me to get Corps HQ to send the Germans over and asked how long they would be. I had hardly put down the telephone when Monty rang. 'Send for Joe Ewart,' he said calmly, 'and tell him we want him here straight away.' Joe, a full colonel who spoke perfect German, was number two to Bill Williams at the Intelligence Office and a key figure in interpreting top-secret Enigma information for Monty. Joe arrived about half an hour later and, shortly after, the German contingent appeared, escorted by a fellow from Corps HQ. 'Line them up, line them up,' Monty said, when I informed him they were here, 'and tell me who they are.'

General Kinzel signs the surrender document. (Eton College Library)

150

Monty and Ewart (standing to Monty's right) and the German delegation in the tent.
(Eton College Library)

Monty kept them waiting for about five minutes and then emerged from his caravan, dressed in battledress and a beret. He had taken the trouble to change out of his customary corduroys and grey sweater for this important occasion. 'Now,' he said, 'who have we got here?' General-Admiral von Friedeburg, the Commander-in-Chief of the German Navy, quickly identified himself and gave the names of his three accomplices. They were General Kinzel, who was Field Marshal Busch's Chief of Staff; Rear Admiral Wagner; and a staff officer, Major Friedl. Colonel Pollok, another staff officer, later joined the party.

Von Friedeburg then told Monty that Hitler was dead and that he had come on behalf of Dönitz, who was now in charge, to negotiate the German surrender. Monty then asked if this was to be a total surrender of all the armed forces, including the Army, Navy and Air Force. Von Friedeburg said that he had not been given any authority to surrender the Navy. Monty replied that he would not accept a part-surrender and told the general-admiral to go away and return only when he had authority to sign for all the German armed forces. So von Friedeburg and Friedl went off in their open Mercedes, accompanied by Trumbull Warren. Kinzel, Wagner and Pollek, however, remained at our HQ.

Left to right:
General-Admiral
von Friedeburg, Rear
Admiral Wagner and
General Kinzel before
the former went by car
to see Dönitz. (Eton
College Library)

Instrument of Surrender

of

All German armed forces in HOLLAND, in

northwest Germany including all islands,

and in DENMARK

1. The German Command agrees to the surrender of all German armed forces in HOLLAND, in northwest GERMANY including the FRISIAN ISLANDS and HELIGOLAND and all other islands, in SCHLESWIG-HOLSTEIN, and in DENMARK, to the C.-in-C. 21 Army Group. This to include all naval ships in these areas. These forces to lay down their arms and to surrender unconditionally.

2. All hostilities on land, on sea, or in the air by German forces in the above areas to cease at 0800 hrs. British Double Summer Time on Saturday 5 May 1945.

3. The German command to carry out at once, and without argument or comment, all further orders that will be issued by the Allied Powers on any subject.

4. Disobedience of orders, or failure to comply with them, will be regarded as a breach of these surrender terms and will be dealt with by the Allied Powers in accordance with the accepted laws and usages of war.

5. This instrument of surrender is independent of, without prejudice to, and will be superseded by any general instrument of surrender imposed by or on behalf of the Allied Powers and applicable to Germany and the German armed forces as a whole.

6. This instrument of surrender is written in English and in German.

   The English version is the authentic text.

7. The decision of the Allied Powers will be final if any doubt or dispute arises as to the meaning or interpretation of the surrender terms.

B. L. Montgomery
Field-Marshal.

Friedeburg

Kinsel

Wagner

Pollek

Friedl

BLM
4ᵗʰ May 1945

1830 hours

The Instrument of Surrender document that Monty sent back to be retyped.
(Eton College Library)

Monty seemed extremely unruffled, but it is easy to imagine the excitement within our camp. We awaited the Germans' return nervously, but there was no emotion at dinner that night.

Von Friedeburg and Friedl got back to our HQ at about half past five in the evening the next day. The rest of the story has been told in many books. But, not so well known is the fact that Monty, who was the first to sign the original surrender document, suddenly exclaimed 'This does not include any reference to the Navy'. He then wrote the words 'This to include all naval ships in these areas' in ink close to the bottom of the first paragraph. He handed me the bit of paper and said, 'Johnny, get this re-typed'. This I did, but I kept the original, which only Monty had signed. It is now in the College Library at Eton, which houses all my wartime photograph books and papers.

At 6.30 p.m. on 4 May 1945, the historic Instrument of Surrender was finally signed on a trestle table covered by an army blanket in a specially erected tent. A sad postscript to this momentous event was that three of the five German officers, who were signatories, were dead within a fortnight. Von Friedeburg poisoned himself; Kinzel went to bed with his blonde mistress and then shot her and himself; and Friedl was killed in a car crash soon after.

SEVEN

THE CHALLENGES OF PEACE

After the armistice, the Allies divided Germany into four separate zones, with Britain, the United States, the USSR and France occupying and administering one each. Berlin was also split similarly into four sectors. By mid-July 1945, when the victorious political leaders met at the Potsdam Conference in the Berlin suburbs, military government was already well established. There was little day-to-day liaison over policy with the Russians, which often made things difficult, but the three other Allies maintained close links and worked well together.

From May 1945 until April 1946, Monty acted as military governor of the British sector in the north-west of occupied Germany and British Control Commissioner for Berlin. While Monty was in charge of the British Zone, the disbandment of the German Army proceeded and sufficient men were discharged to bring in the harvest in the summer of 1945. Coal production was increased and the fishing industry was also revived to produce more much-needed food. However, the disposal of over a million displaced persons, who had mostly fled from the Red Army as it crossed eastern Germany and eastern Europe; the one and three quarter million German prisoners, held in the British Zone; and occasional disagreements with Marshal Zhukov, the governor of the Russian Zone, ensured that Monty's job was far from easy.

Monty departed from Germany in May 1946 and returned to London to head the British Army as CIGS. I did not remain with him much longer and left the Army that July.

Monty visits Berlin's Brandenburg Gate with Marshal Zhukov (holding the envelope in his right hand). (Eton College Library)

The streamers are out in Copenhagen as Monty is driven through the streets to a rapturous welcome. (Eton College Library)

Copenhagen

The first European capital Monty visited after the war ended was Copenhagen. We were met at the airport in an open car and driven through the streets. The whole city was heaving with cheering crowds and jubilant people seemed to be hanging out of every window. Monty was presented with a trophy in the city hall and then we were taken to the Amalienborg Palace for lunch.

I was given a room to freshen up in, which contained a washbasin and the most wonderful Copenhagen chamber pot. I don't know if the equipment in Monty's room was any more modern. But, after lunch was over, we were driven back to the airport and, unfortunately, Monty was sick in the car. When he got out, Monty apologised to the driver for the mess he had made. The chauffeur replied, 'It is an honour, Sir.'

A few years ago, when I was Lord-Lieutenant of Berkshire, I met Queen Margrethe of Denmark when she came to the Royal Military Academy at Sandhurst to take the passing-out parade. She asked me if I had ever been to Copenhagen. I said that I had and told her the story of the beautiful pot. She laughed and assured me that the plumbing arrangements in the royal palace were now more up to date.

Marshal Rokossovsky's Hospitality

Monty had accepted an invitation to lunch with Marshal Rokossovsky at the HQ of the White Russian Army Group in the Russian Zone on 10 May. As I was going back to England on that day, Monty told me to find a liaison officer to accompany him. When I entered their area in our Tac HQ, the first person I saw was John Sharp. I asked if he would like to go: John replied that he would love to.

As usual the Russians provided lots of food and a plentiful supply of vodka. John helped himself liberally throughout the proceedings. After a march past and a demonstration ride by a group of Cossacks, Monty was driven back to the aerodrome, where the Russians fired a 21-gun salute in his honour. John, who by now was extremely inebriated, pulled out his revolver and joined in. Of course, after John had fired six shots, only a series of clicks emanated from his now empty pistol! Poor John

The Cossack parade. (Eton College Library)

was immediately ushered away and locked in the plane's lavatory, where he remained for the flight home.

Monty's version in his memoirs of the story of John's unruly behaviour is a little different to the one I heard, but the end result was much the same. The next day Monty summoned John to his office and told him that he was going to be demoted from the rank of major and sent back to his regiment.

Anyhow, the punishment did John little harm. Monty ordered that he should be given command of a battery as soon as possible, which would automatically make him a major again. Additionally, he never made an official report of the incident. Sure enough, John was soon promoted and eventually ended up as a general.

Monty loved telling this tale, and it provides a good example of how human he was.

The hospitable Marshal Rokossovsky (centre) with Monty. (Eton College Library)

Fan Mail

Monty had always received a slow stream of fan mail, but it rose to a torrent after the war. Every day a huge pile of letters arrived. We were always moved by the correspondence from mothers and wives of soldiers killed in action. The vast majority of letters had to be answered and that kept us busy. I recall there were also one or two from ambitious ladies with proposals of marriage to Monty. After some thought, we came to the conclusion that they did not warrant a reply!

Paris

Monty went over to Paris on 25 May to receive the Grand Cross of the Legion of Honour from de Gaulle. Before he was given France's most famous military decoration, he laid a wreath at the foot of the Arc

Monty receives the Grand Cross of the Legion of Honour from de Gaulle in Les Invalides.
(Eton College Library)

Sir Alan (A.P.) Herbert (foreground), one of Monty's closest friends.
(Eton College Library)

de Triomphe. As we turned to drive back down the Champs-Élysées, the crowds were pavement-thick, as in Copenhagen, and the noise was amazing. The ceremony itself, in the middle of the cobbled courtyard of Les Invalides, which included a magnificent escort of French cavalry horses, was also unforgettable. I still have a vivid mental picture of the huge contrast between the tiny Monty and the extremely tall de Gaulle. It was an extraordinary sight.

We stayed with the British Ambassador, Duff Cooper, and Sir Alan Herbert, who had travelled over to Paris as Monty's guest, accompanied some of us to the Folies Bergères after dinner at the embassy. Just after midnight, A.P.H. suddenly remembered he had not written his column for the *Sunday Mirror*, which was required early the next day. So he got hold of a nightclub programme with a picture of two naked girls on the

front and quickly composed an amusing poem on the back. The first
two lines went as follows:

Enfant Montgomery,
Vous avez pris Paris.

Later we sent the impromptu ditty to the newspaper to ensure that their famous correspondent met his deadline. A.P.H. also made a splendid remark the next morning when we were having a cup of tea before leaving the embassy. 'The damn stuff's corked!' he exclaimed as he took his first sip.

Prague

We flew into Prague on our whis-tle-stop tour of European capitals in late May and were met by the Czechoslovakian President, Eduard Beneš, and the Foreign Minister, Jan Masaryk. That evening we were taken to a performance of *The Bartered Bride* at the State Opera House. When Monty entered his box in the theatre, there was a stand-ing ovation and the whole audience applauded tumultuously.

After the opera the Foreign Minister, who had been the Czech ambassador in London before the war, asked if I would like to join some of his staff for a drink, but warned me to be careful of Russian guards who were everywhere. When we got to the flat of the fellow who was giving the drinks party, a look-out was stationed outside the door to keep an eye out for prowling Red Army soldiers. I was amazed how

Beneš, Masaryk and Monty.
(Eton College Library)

frightened they were of the Russians, who were, after all, their recent liberators and allies.

Next day, we visited the famous church of St Nicholas and attended a huge dinner in the evening. Then there was a reception at the Old Palace before we flew back to Germany on the following day.

During the reception, Monty was talking to Dr Beneš, when a waiter arrived with a tray containing a decanter of sherry, two glasses, and a couple of medals. Monty raised his hand to decline the offer of a drink. So the waiter moved on to me. After I accepted a glass, the man gestured towards the medals. I selected the prettiest one and took it off the tray. Not long after, the waiter returned and informed me that I had picked up the Grand Cross that was meant for Monty. Sadly, I had to return the most distinguished of Czech military awards and take the less important decoration, which was a mere boy's medal. I said to myself, 'That is the nearest you shall ever get to having the Grand Cross of any country in your hand.'

The Wrong Admiral

On 3 June Monty's Tac HQ moved back to Ostenwalde in Lower Saxony where it had been previously located for a few days on the advance through Germany. Ostenwalde was a beautiful Schloss with many well-furnished rooms. There was also a large lake within its glorious grounds. We stayed in this idyllic place near Osnabrück for a year until Monty went back to England to become CIGS.

I recall an amusing incident that occurred during my time at Ostenwalde. A new admiral, who had been appointed to our HQ, was coming to meet Monty for the first time. It was four in the afternoon and pouring with rain when a man in a large cover coat with no badges or markings on the shoulders arrived. I thought it was the admiral who was due then. So I showed him into Monty's office and went back to my own tent.

As I approached the tent, to my horror I noticed a distinguished naval officer in full uniform with gold braid all over his arms. 'Are you the admiral?' I asked nervously.

Dinner at Ostenwalde for officers and men of Tac HQ. (Eton College Library)

When he answered in the affirmative, I said, 'One moment please.' To avert the crisis, I rushed off and sent a note in to Monty, saying, 'This is the wrong admiral. The right one is outside!'

When I ushered the genuine admiral into Monty's caravan, the other man stepped out, looking rather bemused. I apologised for misidentifying him and he told me that he was actually the dentist. Feeling very embarrassed, I hurried off to find the poor fellow whose tooth he had come to extract.

I heard later that Monty was not amused by my mistake.

Ostenwalde Schloss, Monty's base in Germany after the war. (Henderson)

The White Stallion

Not long after we returned to Ostenwalde, a white Arab stallion, once owned by Rommel, was brought to the Schloss's stables where there were already a few German horses and grooms. The stallion, which we also named 'Rommel', had a hazy recent past, as nobody seemed to know what had happened to him after his owner committed suicide when the plot to kill the Führer failed. But the 'Desert Fox' had reputedly acquired him earlier in North Africa to ride in triumph into Cairo. Later, when Hitler recalled Rommel to Europe, the stallion, which had sustained minor injuries in an air raid, was apparently transported back to France to recuperate.

When Monty, who had twice thwarted Rommel's ambitions to take Cairo at Alam Halfa and Alamein, heard about the stallion's

A nervous Monty aboard 'Rommel'. (Eton College Library)

extraordinary history, he quickly recognised its publicity value and decided to be photographed, mounted on his great rival's horse. Although he had taken part in a jackal hunt at Quetta in Pakistan before the war and, as an infantry officer, needed to ride a charger on occasions, Monty had not been in the saddle for six years or more. So there were

The author puts 'Rommel' through his paces. (Eton College Library)

some very anxious moments when the groom removed the leading rein for the photographer to obtain the appropriate shots. I remember Monty looked absolutely terrified when 'Rommel' broke into nothing more than a leisurely walk.

In fact Monty need not have worried. I used to exercise the stallion every morning in the summer of 1945 and can vouch that he was a delightful conveyance and beautifully behaved.

There was one occasion, though, when the poor horse totally forgot himself and that was not his fault at all. A pompous and bossy brigadier, whom I did not like much, asked if he could take the white stallion for a ride. I am ashamed to say that I arranged for the officer, who was not much of a horseman, to ride out with a groom, who was aboard a mare that was mad in season.

Of course, the stallion soon lost his self-control and began to whinny and rear up on his hind legs. As the terrified brigadier's riding skills were not up to managing such behaviour, he immediately baled out by grabbing hold of a nearby tree. The unfortunate officer was left hanging from a branch, looking extremely undignified, while the love-struck 'Rommel' galloped off in pursuit of the mare.

A Misunderstanding at Potsdam

During the Potsdam Conference, which started on 17 July, Churchill gave a dinner for Stalin and his entourage. As we entered the room, we all shook hands with the Russian leader and his staff. Stalin was a huge, broad fellow, but I remember being struck most by his expressionless face.

Clement Attlee was at our end of the table. Of course, the Labour leader then had no idea that he would win the General Election on 26 July and become the new prime minister.

After dinner, Winston said during his speech, 'What the Russians don't know about warfare isn't worth knowing.' As a double negative

Monty and Stalin. (IWM HU87144)

is never used in the Russian language, Stalin's interpreter had no option but to translate Winston's words, as 'What the Russians don't know about warfare is a lot.'

Stalin looked absolutely amazed, while Winston's interpreter gallantly tried to put things right with his Russian counterpart. Clearly he was not very successful, as in the end Stalin just shrugged his shoulders and Winston had to continue with his speech.

Extra Pay

After Attlee's government came to power in the summer of 1945, there were discussions suggesting that Monty should be given a lump sum as a thank-you for his role in winning the war. The figure being bandied about was the then substantial sum of £125,000.

The government later decided that if Monty received a gift, it would be unfair if eight other top military figures were not endowed with a similar amount. But, sadly, Attlee and his ministers also concluded that a total sum of over a million pounds was too much to extract from the Treasury's coffers in those deprived postwar days.

So Monty ended up with nothing for his Herculean efforts. When one thinks what Marlborough and Wellington received from their country for their great victories, it was incredibly ungrateful.

To Gstaad on Göring's Train

Monty had read in the *Ski Club of Great Britain* journal that his ski boots were displayed in a glass case in a hotel in Lenk in Switzerland's Bernese Oberland. So he told Carol Mather to get them back. During his enquiries, Carol contacted Sir Clifford Norton, the minister at the British Legation in Bern. Sir Clifford kindly arranged for his wife, Peter, an intrepid skier, to collect them. When she first set eyes on the boots, she was amazed to find a pre-war label still attached, with the words 'Colonel B.L. Montgomery' written in the owner's inimitable hand.

After the boots were retrieved, Peter sent Carol off skiing for a few days, and on his return suggested that it would be wonderful for

Monty in his beloved white coat poses with his Swiss guards. (Eton College Library)

The luxurious Chalet Gifferhorn in Gstaad. (Eton College Library)

The author and Carol Mather (right) take to the slopes. Sir Clifford Norton is next to Monty.
(Eton College Library)

Anglo-Swiss relations if Monty paid a visit. Carol agreed to push the idea but privately rather doubted its practicality. However, when he returned to Germany, he found that Monty was recovering from a bout of pneumonia. Carol put Peter's plan to Monty and suggested it would

Monty and Carol Mather enjoy a sleigh ride. (Eton College Library)

do his health some good. To his surprise, the invalid accepted the offer with alacrity. Therefore Carol organised an extended break for Monty's convalescence in Switzerland during February 1946.

When the time came to go, we set off in some style from Germany in Göring's private train. It carried the most amazing collection of classical records of which the Reichsmarschall was reputedly very fond. There was also a special bath, constructed on two levels, in which one sat rather than lay. As the suspension on the German train's carriages went across rather than along the line of the rails, the water in Göring's personal bath never overflowed! We also took several mess staff from our Tac HQ. They had a whale of a time in the private train's luxurious kitchens.

When we reached Switzerland, we stayed for a few days in a hotel. Then we moved on to Gstaad, where the banker, Benjy Guinness, generously lent us his magnificent home, the Chalet Gifferhorn. The chalet had a fantastic chef and we had the most delicious lunch with Benjy on the day we arrived.

Sadly, Benjy could not stay for long, but before he left he showed us a cupboard that was full to the brim with bottles of wine. 'If you need anymore, you will have to get it yourself,' he said with a grin. I have no idea what sort of entertaining our kind host was expecting us to do, but we could never have drunk all that wine in the week that we were there on our own.

Carol and I used to have a bottle of champagne and some delicious canapés sent up to our bathroom each evening. It was sheer bliss lying back in the bath eating and drinking our fill, but we never dared tell Monty about such hedonistic behaviour.

Early on in our visit, when we were about to go up to the mountains, a kind Swiss guard, fearing Monty might feel the cold, lent him a huge white fur coat. Monty really took a shine to this exotic garment and wore it all the time. Towards the end of our stay, the guard asked me to make sure that Monty did not take the coat away. The poor man must have begun to fear that he would never get his prized possession back!

I also remember that the locals asked if they could organise a toot of horns on the mountain for Monty. This was duly arranged and he much enjoyed the concert.

Goodbye to the Rhine Army

I often used to write Monty's speeches, so it was no surprise when he asked me to compose a farewell broadcast to deliver to the soldiers of the Rhine Army just before he left Germany to be CIGS in London in early May 1946.

I used to start by writing the original drafts of his speeches in longhand and then get my text typed up. Monty would read through my handiwork and add his own alterations, additions or deletions in ink. Then I would take the edited version back to the typists, who would make a fair copy.

Once I was experiencing the dreaded writer's block and, hard though I tried, I could not find a suitable start. My problem was suddenly solved when I remembered the initial sentence of H.A.L. Fisher's *History of England from the Accession of Henry VII to the Death of Henry VIII*, which I had read in my schooldays. 'In the hands of strength lie the keys of war and peace' had always seemed to me to be to be a splendid opening line. It was extraordinary, but immediately I wrote those magical

The farewell broadcast to the Rhine Army with Monty's corrections.
(Eton College Library)

words onto the paper, the rest of Monty's speech began to flow easily from my pen.

When Monty eventually read my draft, he congratulated me on its excellent beginning. I was too embarrassed to admit that those stirring words were not my own.

Furnishing the Flat

Monty had lost all his furniture when the warehouse in Portsmouth where it was stored suffered a direct hit from a bomb. So, when he returned to England, he gave me £2,000 to furnish the London flat he had taken in Westminster Gardens, off Marsham Street. The difficulty was that I was required to complete the operation in two days.

First, I paid a visit to an old Eighth Army colleague, who owned a furniture shop in Chiswick. He let me have a dining-room table and a set of chairs quite cheaply as a favour to his old army commander. Then I had to search other shops quickly to obtain a bed and a sofa, which were more expensive. But, as £2,000 was a lot of money in 1946, I was able to buy some quite smart stuff.

Demob

When I left the Army in July, I went round to Monty's flat to say goodbye. I also wanted to retrieve a beautiful hand-made rug that I had purchased the month before in Delhi, while we were visiting the Viceroy of India, Field Marshal Lord Wavell. When we arrived home from India, I asked Monty if I could store my new carpet in his flat as there was no suitable space for it in my own. He said that he was happy to take it to Westminster Gardens.

While Monty and I were chatting away, I noticed the Indian rug in pride of place in front of the fireplace and I must say it certainly brightened up the room. Just before I left, I managed to pluck up enough courage to ask for it back. Monty's face dropped immediately and he said rather meekly, 'Oh Johnny, I thought you had given it to me as a present.' I was struck dumb for a moment, but quickly recovered my composure and decided to stick to my guns, 'No,' I replied, 'I'm sorry if there has been a misunderstanding, but the rug was only meant to be on loan.'

Later, while I was driving home with my Indian acquisition safely rolled up in the boot, I wondered if I had been rather mean to my old chief. But I soon persuaded myself that there were mitigating circumstances. I did not have much money at the time and the rug, which had

Monty greets Wavell. (Eton College Library)

been far too expensive for my low army wages, was then one of my most valuable possessions.

An Unexpected Apology

As I was keen to see the other side of the Atlantic, I agreed to take up my old position with Monty temporarily for a trip to Canada and the United States in the late summer of 1946. We set sail from Liverpool for Canada on 19 August and returned exactly a month later by air from Washington to London.

We had a hectic schedule in Canada, travelling to every province, and then spent a couple of hours with their Prime Minister,

*Monty's letter of thanks to the author for joining him on his
American trip.* (Eton College Library)

Mackenzie King, in Ottawa on our way to the United States on
10 September. In America, Monty stayed with Eisenhower at his
Washington home and rekindled their friendship, had a long talk
with President Truman in the White House and toured several major
military installations. Again there was little time to relax, so Monty
got very tired. Furthermore, as his visit was unofficial, he was under
considerable pressure over what he could and could not say as the new
CIGS. Therefore it was understandable that he became quite irritable
at times as well.

I did not mind, as I had learnt long ago that it was good policy to keep
out of the way in such situations. But it must have preyed on Monty's
conscience that he had given me a hard time. He sent me a letter in
early October, which included an apology for his difficult behaviour
on occasions. I was quite surprised but also touched to discover that he
must have been worrying that our working relationship had ended on
a sour note.

A Touch of Flattery

When Monty published his memoirs in October 1958 he kindly sent me a signed copy, bearing an inscription, which contained the following lines:

> To: Johnny Henderson who marched with me from Alamein to Berlin as my A.D.C., and who never put a foot wrong.

I often wondered if Monty would have written those generous words if he had known about some of the pranks his ADCs perpetrated in North Africa!

The inscription in the author's copy of Monty's memoirs. (Eton College Library)

Nearing the End

Two weeks before Monty died on 24 March 1976 I heard that his health was fading fast. So I telephoned his home at Islington Mill, near Alton in Hampshire, to arrange a visit.

When I eventually arrived, rather flustered after a long and terrible drive in filthy weather conditions, I was taken to Monty's bedroom. As I looked round the door, Monty, who was tucked up in bed, said, 'Johnny, I'm far too tired, far too tired. I can't see you now.' He then closed his eyes and it was clear that my brief audience was over.

As Monty seemed likely to sleep for a long time, I thought there was no point in hanging around. So I quickly left the house and got straight into my car. I had not driven very far, when, strangely, I began to chuckle. I think I was happy to discover that Monty, who was always abrupt and never prevaricated, had not changed at all.

Sadly, that was the last time I ever saw my old boss.

Monty at his home at Islington Mill. (IWM 44417)

A Lasting Memorial

In the late 1970s, after Monty had died, I began to think that there ought to be a statue in London to honour the man who had done so much to defeat the Germans and safeguard the treasured British way of life. I soon found out that many others thought the same. Therefore an organising committee was formed, headed by Field Marshal Lord Harding of Petherton, to persuade the powers-that-be to allocate a position for the statue in Whitehall, the street of government where there are several other sculptures of distinguished military figures.

To cut a long story short, it took some time and a letter to national newspaper editors before we got our way, but it was eventually agreed to find a spot for a statue at the front of the Ministry of Defence, provided that we could raise the money to pay a sculptor. Luckily we managed to drum up enough generous donations, totalling £30,000, to be able to commission Oscar Nemon, one of the most famous sculptors of the time. He produced a wonderful likeness, which received much critical acclaim, and the huge bronze of Monty, wearing his customary army beret, was unveiled at a memorable ceremony by Queen Elizabeth the Queen Mother in 1980.

That was not the end of the saga, however. In late 1981 I was surprised to receive a letter from the Department of the Environment, saying that the statue needed cleaning and asking for a one-off payment of £16,000 from our committee to ensure its maintenance in

The mandarin's warning letter.
(Eton College Library)

perpetuity. I thought the request was pretty cheeky and wrote back to the D of E to that effect. But, as the bronze by now was looking very grubby, I also decided to get a move on and organise the initial cleaning myself. So, rather than pay inflated London prices, I sent two estate workers from my home near Newbury to do the job.

Their arrival caused quite a stir among the Whitehall police and the Ministry's security staff when they first unloaded their buckets and brooms from the van. But they were allowed to proceed after they presented their credentials. It did not take the men long to remove the calling cards of London's pigeons and the city grime, and Monty's memorial was soon in pristine condition again.

Happily, my letter of complaint to the D of E and the subsequent cleaning operation soon had the desired result. I received a reply from the Ministry, dated 8 January 1982, informing our committee that, in

The unveiling of Monty's statue in Whitehall by Queen Elizabeth, The Queen Mother.
(IWM HU87151)

future, the annual cost of maintaining the statue would: 'be found from Departmental funds'.

I had to laugh, though, when I read the next few lines:

'I need hardly add that Treasury have agreed to this as an exceptional measure in the particular case of the statue of Lord Montgomery and their decision is not intended to set a precedent for public statues generally. I say this not because I expect you

The author in front of his home at West Woodhay. (Henderson family)

will ever be involved in organising another public statue but so that the record may be straight.'

He may have said the opposite in his letter, but I have always thought that the mandarin had been instructed by his nervous superiors to make sure that I did not try to put up any more monuments in London!

EPILOGUE

Just as he forecast to Monty at dinner in the North African desert, Johnny Henderson went into the City after leaving the army as a major in 1946. He joined Cazenove & Co., the famous stockbroker, into which a family firm, Greenwood Henderson, had been merged in 1932. Johnny quickly showed an appetite and aptitude for his chosen profession and was made a partner after only eight years. He remained at Cazenove for thirty-six years until his retirement in 1982.

Johnny gained a reputation in the Square Mile as a shrewd spotter of lucrative opportunities for his clients, which sometimes included less traditional investments, such as agricultural land or, a particular favourite of his, wine. He was also deemed to be a good judge of character and therefore soon became one of the partners responsible for selecting new employees. When the pension fund industry took off in the 1950s and '60s, he was a leading light in building relationships with their fund managers, which gave Cazenove its enviable placing power for share issues. On a lighter note, he made many entries in the partners' betting book, once even wagering on how many cherry stones a fellow luncher left on his plate!

Johnny also held other important positions in the City. In 1978 he became chairman of Henderson Administration, the fund manager originally established in the 1930s to look after the holdings of his grandfather, Harry Henderson, and his great uncle, Alexander, the first Lord Faringdon, who had made their fortunes financing the building of railways in Spain and Argentina. Furthermore, he was a long-serving director of Barclays Bank and chairman of its trust company.

In addition, Johnny was an influential figure in the horseracing world. He was well known as a Jockey Club member, owner, breeder, amateur jockey and as the father of the leading National Hunt trainer Nicky Henderson. But his greatest legacy was to lend his financial expertise to a sport not previously renowned for good housekeeping. He was a major player in the creation of the Racecourse Holdings Trust, a non-profit-making organisation that saved several courses in the less solvent age before valuable television and radio contracts.

When Cheltenham was threatened by a property developers' takeover, Johnny was the financial brain who brought together a pro-racing group of investors to buy the Mecca of jumping for £240,000 in 1963. As a direct result, the RHT, which now owns thirteen courses, including Newmarket and Aintree, was set up the following year. Ten years later, Johnny and his fellow subscribers sold their shares in the body at a nominal price to the Turf's then ruling body, the Jockey Club, with the proviso that all RHT revenues should always be ploughed back into racing.

Cheltenham later gratefully acknowledged Johnny's enormous contribution towards safeguarding its future. He was their patron until his death, and the course has now rightly renamed a race on the last day of its renowned March Festival, the Johnny Henderson Grand Annual Chase Challenge Cup.

Johnny will go down in history as one of the saviours of Britain's two most famous jumping tracks, Cheltenham and Aintree, but he also helped secure the future of the jewel in flat racing's crown, Ascot. He was a trustee of the Berkshire course from 1973 to 1985, when it was still suffering the financial effects of a huge redevelopment programme in the 1960s. Johnny initiated a sinking fund to set aside income to pay off that debt which became the foundation stone for the even bigger rebuilding undertaking that started at Ascot in the autumn of 2004.

He was appointed MBE in 1944 and OBE and CVO in 1985. He was also Lord-Lieutenant of Berkshire and, aptly, as nobody was friendlier or more gregarious, chairman of White's club in St James's. Johnny was also instrumental in persuading several of his Eton schoolfellows to become involved in the acclaimed private publication of the letters of their housemaster's wife, Grizel Hartley, who had been a huge influence on him and his contemporaries in their formative years.

In 1949 he married Sarah Beckwith-Smith, with whom he had two sons, Nicky, and Harry, who followed his father into Cazenove, and a daughter, Josie. Sarah died tragically in a hunting accident in 1972 and Johnny married for a second time in 1976, Catherine Christian, who had a son and two daughters from a previous marriage.

Johnny only decided to write the tale of his time as Monty's ADC in the summer of 2003. He worked diligently and with great zest on the book, until he passed away suddenly at the age of 83 on 16 December 2003 at his home at West Woodhay, near Newbury. Fortunately, he left enough material for his last big project to be completed.

ACKNOWLEDGEMENTS

Johnny Henderson sadly did not live to see the memoirs of his time as Monty's ADC published, but he would have wanted me to acknowledge the following for enabling *Watching Monty* to happen.

Many thanks are due to Sir Carol Mather, Johnny's old friend and army colleague, for checking the typescript, giving much sound advice, and writing a perceptive foreword; Monty's son, David, the 2nd Viscount Montgomery of Alamein, for reading and commenting on the text and for kindly allowing items, which are his copyright, to be reproduced; Christopher Dowling of the Imperial War Museum for his help in finding a publisher and for persuading the museum to take part in the venture; Michael Meredith and Nick Baker of the Eton College Library, where Johnny's collection of wartime memorabilia is stored, for spending so much time, scanning and photographing numerous albums and documents; and Jonathan Falconer of Sutton Publishing for his invaluable assistance and for persuading his directors to take on the book.

I must also thank Johnny's widow, Catherine, and his children, Nicky, Harry and Josie, for encouraging me to complete the work.

Last but not least, I would like to express much gratitude to Johnny for asking me to collaborate on his project. Working with him was the greatest fun and it was fascinating to hear his side of the Monty story. I hope he would have approved of the end result.

Jamie Douglas-Home

INDEX

Note: italic page numbers indicate illustrations.